Meaningful Coincidence

*Remarkable true stories of synchronicity
and the search for answers*

Jan Cederquist

Marshall Cavendish
Editions

Copyright © 2010 Jan Cederquist

First published in Swedish in 2005 by Bokförlaget Langenskiöld as
Slumpen är ingen tillfällighet

First published in English in 2010 by Marshall Cavendish Editions
An imprint of Marshall Cavendish International

5F / 32–38 Saffron Hill
London EC1N 8FH
United Kingdom

and

1 New Industrial Road
Singapore 536196
genrefsales@sg.marshallcavendish.com
www.marshallcavendish.com/genref

Marshall Cavendish is a trademark of Times Publishing Limited

Other Marshall Cavendish offices:
Marshall Cavendish International (Asia) Private Limited, 1 New Industrial Road,
Singapore 536196 • Marshall Cavendish Corporation. 99 White Plains Road,
Tarrytown NY 10591–9001, USA • Marshall Cavendish International (Thailand)
Co Ltd. 253 Asoke, 12th Floor, Sukhumvit 21 Road, Klongtoey Nua, Wattana,
Bangkok 10110, Thailand • Marshall Cavendish (Malaysia) Sdn Bhd, Times
Subang, Lot 46, Subang Hi-Tech Industrial Park, Batu Tiga, 40000 Shah Alam,
Selangor Darul Ehsan, Malaysia

A CIP record for this book is available from the British Library

ISBN 978-0-462-09970-5

Printed and bound in Great Britain by
CPI William Clowes, Beccles NR34 7TL

To my parents Ida and Sven Cederquist,
who always kept a window open

"Every coincidence," said Miss Marple to herself, "is always worth
noticing. Later one can throw it away, if it was just a coincidence."
Agatha Christie

Jan Cederquist was one of the most successful copywriters in Sweden, and a leader in the field of Swedish advertising. His list of domestic and international creative awards is longer than most. Yet he still found time to pursue his keen interest in philosophy, psychology and spiritual matters.

He left the advertising industry in 1994 to devote his time to his main interests – writing, gardening and playing jazz on his double bass.

Jan was married with four children and lived in Lidingo, an island suburb of Stockholm. He died in 2009.

Contents

Foreword / vii

1   It happens to you too / 1

2   *And there sat Gunnar* / 6

3   *And there stood the police* / 9

4   Are coincidences statistical or mystical? / 12

5   *The scarab and the grand piano* / 18

6   Is now the time? / 21

7   *Old boats* / 29

8   *Is there a doctor out there?* / 32

9   *The double bass and the therapist* / 35

10 *The apartment* / 42

11 What is it are a part of? / 45

12 *Gustaf and Kim* / 52

13 *The dream woman* / 56

14 Global Consciousness Project / 59

15 *The outboard motor and the cash register* / 62

16 *Fredrik's pictures* / 64

17 *Just an idea* / 68

18 *The accelerator* / 72

19 *The confirmation* / 75

20 Cause and effect / 81

Contents

21   *The road to Bäckastrand* / 86
22   *Three problems – one solution* / 93
23   Can you evoke synchronicities? / 104
24   *The right colour* / 108
25   *The floor man* / 111
26   Project Stargate / 114
27   *The concrete man* / 117
28   *The bass players' world* / 122
29   What do we know? / 125
30   *The actor and the murderer* / 128
31   *The postcard man* / 130
32   Morphic fields / 135
33   *"Basin Street Blues"* / 138
34   The big question / 142
35   *The Bermuda triangle* / 147
36   *The IKEA man* / 150
37   Everything is connected to everything else / 155
38   *Say it with music* / 157
39   *Small coincidences* / 163
40   *Synchronicity and the Bible* / 168
41   Intuition / 171
42   *The struggle between intuition and intellect* / 176
43   *How I quit smoking without even trying* / 179
44   *The return of the contact lens* / 182
45   *Father and son* / 185
46   Pieces of the puzzle / 188
47   *Where are we heading?* / 193
48   *Two wolves* / 198

Further reading / 199

Foreword

Finding the objective truth has long been the highest goal of Western science.

Investigating, probing, analysing. Black or white, true or false, right or wrong. That is how we are used to categorizing the phenomena of our existence. That which does not fit into the pattern is often not taken seriously.

Just as science has had a monopoly on the truth, religion has had a monopoly on spirituality. But today we are beginning to see many examples of spirituality without religious connotations. Or, perhaps more accurately, a spirituality expressed with words from beyond the world of religions.

Quantum physicists, psychologists and philosophers are beginning to find ways of getting closer to each other. "Synchronicity" is such a concept. The term was coined by Carl Gustaf Jung in the 1920s, but has now achieved a renewed currency. It signifies a non-causal connection between two or more events that are simultaneous or related to each other in a meaningful way.

Seek and you shall find! But only that which you seek. Empirical science, rooted in Aristotle, especially since Newton, has been based on the assumption that everything follows causal laws. It has also been extremely successful in mapping such connections. But as one seldom finds what one does not seek or expect, the possible alternative patterns have hardly been noticed. Only since the breakthrough of quantum physics has it become obvious that the Newtonian paradigm is insufficient to describe, and even less to explain, the deep structures of existence.

Today we know that it is not always possible to uphold the split between subject and object, observer and observed. Instead the viewer is part of and influences that which is being viewed, regardless of whether it is the smallest building blocks of existence or our own consciousness that is being studied.

A central hypothesis of Jung's concerned a collective subconscious in the depth of our souls. It connects us with each other and opens up an often unconscious and intuitive, non-verbal communication between people. This collective subconscious also contains certain common patterns and symbols, the so-called archetypes, unrestricted by time and space.

The physicists of today have arrived, from totally different angles, at a point where it seems necessary to count on more dimensions than space and time. The possibility of a dimension of non-time and non-space could theoretically make possible a meeting between past, present and future, and also make spatial distances irrelevant. Perhaps the notion of a collective unconscious, independent of time and space, might also clear the path for a new understanding of the central assumption in religion of an existence beyond the visible.

The more we know, the more we understand how little we know. But what we know for sure is that we are just at the beginning of an exciting journey of consciousness. Perhaps, after all, coincidences do not happen just by chance. This book gives us several thought-provoking examples that can teach us to see our own existence with curious, newly opened eyes.

Bishop Lennart Koskinen

1   It happens to you too

People travel to wonder at the height of mountains,
at the huge waves of the sea,
at the long courses of rivers,
at the vast compass of the ocean,
at the circular motion of the stars;
and they pass by themselves without wondering.

St Augustine

Everybody has experienced a strange meeting or a strange occurrence of some kind in their life. For example, you decide to call a certain person, but just as you reach for the telephone it rings and it is that very person. We have words that help us avoid thinking more deeply about such things. "Chance," we say. It was "by pure chance", and life goes on as if nothing has happened.

Or you are in the department store and suddenly you begin thinking of someone you have not seen for a long time. At that very moment he or she comes down the escalator. That funny "chance" again. We might be a bit startled temporarily, but to regain our peace of mind we quickly banish our wonderment to the murky lumber room of our consciousness and forget about it.

I cannot do that any more.

That "chance" has popped up too many times in my life. It has shown me a way, provided a solution or saved me from a troubling situation. It has to a large degree influenced my life, sometimes even with a humorous twinkle in the eye. Time after time things have happened that, according to statistical probabilities should not have happened, things that mathematically and scientifically are totally improbable, not to say impossible. But still they have handed me meaningful, often elegant, solutions to problems big and small.

That is why I no longer believe in "chance". Not the kind of chance one usually talks about when saying "it happened by pure chance". That which is considered nothing more than a kind of statistical air pocket, something that just happens without meaning and there is nothing more to it.

I have begun to suspect that there is a lot more to it. I have become more and more convinced that chance is something quite other that what we have been led to believe. I have begun to realize that chance is no coincidence.

The legendary psychiatrist Carl Jung was very interested in coincidences and coined the word *synchronicity* for *meaningful coincidence*. He thought that there might be some kind of connection between synchronicity and intuition. It seems as if everything in the universe is permeated with some kind of underlying order, or intelligence, or whatever it is – something that I am deeply curious about, an oddity that I would like to share with you in this book. I would simply like to tell you about strange things that have actually happened, and invite you as a reader to share my amazement at how fantastic and remarkable life really is.

I once had the privilege of meeting quantum physicist Fritjof Capra, who has written several bestselling books such as *The Tao of Physics* and *The Turning Point*. Fritjof explained that science usually involves formulating an hypothesis about something one wants to investigate, then designing and carrying out experiments that will either confirm or confute that hypothesis.

"But now," he said, "now things are happening in our laboratories that we don't even have any hypothesis about. We simply cannot understand what sometimes happens and why."

In other words, we live as humans in a universe we can only understand to a very small extent. Most of it is still unknown. So what is it really that we are a part of during our journey between the cradle and the grave, this enormously remarkable episode we call life? Most reflecting people do sometimes wonder what it is all about. Who am I? What is the meaning of my life? What is my role in the universe? Where was I before I was born and where do I go when I die?

Often it is no more than a vague thought that just very lightly touches our consciousness. Many people will even find such thoughts unpleasant and brush them away like a wasp at the garden tea table. I have heard people say: "Hell, no, don't brood over that kind of stuff, you'll just go crazy." We would rather immerse ourselves in the everyday goings-on in life – the job, the family, the house, the golf, the car, and everything else that demands our daily attention. Of course we have to deal with those things. It is quite natural and necessary since they are a part of the material reality in which we live.

But I cannot help wondering, and I have become more and more convinced that there actually does exist a greater reality beyond the one we can see and touch.

Perhaps *synchronicity* is a reminder of the big mystery we

are a part of? Fritjof said synchronistic events could emanate from a kind of resonance or interplay between patterns in consciousness and patterns in matter. I was all ears. Here was one of the world's best-known physicists suggesting that there might be a connection between mind and matter, between a person's thoughts and feelings and what happens in the world outside him or herself, and that synchronicity could be a connection between these two worlds.

Synchronicity is nowadays gaining more and more attention as a curious but hard-to-explain aspect of life. To me it is a fascinating curiosity. My own synchronistic experiences, and those others have shared with me, have convinced me that we are dealing with something that is much bigger and stranger than we understand at this point. Stranger than we can imagine – perhaps even stranger than our minds can embrace.

I am neither a scientist nor a priest and I do not strive for scientific stringency or religious decorum. And I do not believe that I am specifically chosen, or that I suffer from what is called a "grandiose personality disturbance". I am just a curious layman who has developed the habit of noticing when strange things happen, and who cannot refrain from wondering what it is all about.

I would therefore like to encourage you, dear reader, to pay attention to similar occurrences in your own life. Synchronicity happens to everyone. Next time it happens to you, take it to heart, look at it and see what it really contains. Maybe there is something of value to you. If nothing else I promise that life will become more interesting, more fun and more exciting.

Is there a greater adventure than that which we call life? That big enigma, that strange and unfathomable mystery that no scientist in the world can explain to us. Nobody knows. But it is fascinating to speculate and to dig for answers.

As Milan Kundera says in *The Unbearable Lightness of Being*: "Thus it is wrong to criticize the novel for paying attention to peculiar coincidences. But it is right to criticize man for being blind to coincidences in his daily life, because then he deprives himself of a dimension of beauty."

Not only beauty.

2 *And there sat Gunnar*

Something had happened at the advertising agency and I didn't know how to handle the situation. I had recently been appointed CEO of the company and had to do something, but what? I did not have a lot of experience as CEO. Coming from the creative side, I was pretty ignorant of the economic system, and I had a strong need to discuss the situation with an experienced person.

There was such a person. Gunnar Wessman had been CEO of several well-known Swedish corporations, such as Perstorp, Uddeholm and Pharmacia. He was now retired, but his solid business background and understanding of people were a good support for me as I tried to handle a job I had only accepted with some hesitation.

We met occasionally and talked about big and small issues. Gunnar had become a kind of mentor, and now I really needed to see him urgently. But unfortunately that was not possible. He had a tight travel schedule and there was simply no time for a meeting at such short notice.

I felt stressed and worried, especially since the issue was not really suited to a discussion over the phone. All I needed was an hour face to face with Gunnar, but no such luck. It hung over me like a low pressure system in November. Besides, in the middle of it all I suddenly had to rush to a totally unrelated business meeting in Copenhagen.

I got into my car that morning and left home for Arlanda Airport. As I approached the Lidingö bridge I became vaguely aware of something happening on the bridge. In front of me was a grey Volvo, whose driver suddenly hit the brakes. So did I, and I barely managed to stop without hitting him. He had in turn just managed to stop without getting entangled in what was happening in front of him, a line of seven or eight cars all bumping into each other.

There did not seem to be any serious damage or personal injuries, just some dented bumpers, broken lights and glass splinters on the road. I saw no reason for me to stick around, so I carefully pulled over into the other lane to pass the accident. After all, I did not want to miss my flight.

As I slowly passed the grey Volvo that had stopped in front of me, the door opened and a man got out.

It was Gunnar!

I made an unsuccessful attempt to get his attention, but traffic urged me on from behind and I had to get to Arlanda. I realized that it would have been impossible anyway to have a chat there and then. Shit! So close and yet so far. I really needed to talk to him, but had to drive on.

Having checked in at the airport I buried myself in a newspaper. It was a bit difficult to focus on the pages. Thoughts of my job problems, of Gunnar and the collisions on the bridge constantly got in the way. Eventually the loudspeakers announced it was time for departure. People immediately hurried to the exit gate, just to get stuck there in a rapidly growing line. It happens all the time. As soon there is even a scratch over the loudspeaker passengers become extremely anxious to get on board. Why this haste, considering that you usually have your seat marked on the boarding pass? I took it easy, kept on reading and waited till the worst crowding was over. I really needed no more stress at this point. Trying to be relaxed, I showed my boarding pass at the control desk and comfortably strolled aboard looking for my seat. I had seat 8B.

When I got there I suddenly felt dizzy.

In seat 8A sat Gunnar!

3 *And there stood the police*

It was a reasonably mild collision. My business partner, Lars Hall, and I were cruising in my company car, a brown Peugeot 506, along a narrow street in Stockholm. Approaching an intersection, I slowed down a bit more, since visibility to the right was rather poor. But apparently I was not careful enough. A black car came tearing out from nowhere and there was a bang, and since he had come from the right it was clearly my fault.

Lars and I got out of the car, fortunately unharmed. From the other car emerged two Asian men in military uniforms. One of the uniforms was fairly simple, black and without decorations. The other was more impressive, with golden threads, buttons and medals. They proved to be the military attaché (an admiral) at the Thai embassy and his very embarrassed chauffeur.

We looked at the dented bumpers and broken headlights. I began apologizing, prepared to plead guilty and start filling out the insurance papers. But the admiral waved his hand – it was a mere trifle, nobody was hurt, nothing to worry about. "No problem, no problem." He apparently wanted to get out of there as quickly as possible. We shook hands, smiled apologetically at each other, exchanged some pleasantries and agreed to forget the whole thing. Shit happens. Our friendliness was probably augmented by the fact that none of us would have to pay for the repairs out of our own pockets.

The damage to my car was not so bad that I couldn't drive away from the scene. But I fretted a bit over all the hassle involved in getting it to a garage, filling out insurance papers and all the rest.

But suddenly it struck me. I remembered that I already had a booking for a service at the garage – the very next morning! It doesn't happen very often that you are involved in a collision, and it doesn't happen very often that you have a booking at a garage. But here both things happened within twelve hours. Lars and I joked about the perfect timing of this collision.

It would get even better. The next morning I left home for the 35-kilometre drive into town and the planned visit to the garage. I was amused at my luck, and the coincidence that meant that the garage were ready to take care of my car this very morning.

But after a few kilometres I noticed something very unpleasant. The temperature needle was pointing to red! I realized that the radiator must have been damaged in the collision and that the coolant had trickled out during the night. Goddamn it! That's what I got from sitting there being so smug. I had just entered a stretch of the road that goes through an uninhabited area, with nothing but trees, just woodland, for several kilometres.

My thoughts were racing. I must stop immediately. I can't drive with an overheated engine, it could seize up at any moment. What to do now? How do I get hold of a breakdown van? (There was no telephone available for miles; it was just before the era of the mobile phone.) I must try to get the attention of some other car passing by to get a ride. Embarrassing to stand here at the roadside waving my hands. Why did it have to happen just here, on this deserted stretch of the road? What had happened to my good luck? It must have run out now.

I was pretty upset and afraid that the engine would be damaged. But at the same time it was as if one part of my awareness quite calmly just observed the other part that was so upset sitting there in the car.

The next moment I saw something that I had never seen during the fifteen years I had been driving along this road almost daily – a police control point!

A policeman stood by the roadside waving a stop sign. It is probably the only time in my life that I have felt relief and joy at being stopped at a police control. Usually I immediately feel a vague, unspecified sense of guilt. Am I sober, do I have my driving licence and so on. But now, with a happy feeling of surprise and relief, I pulled over to the roadside, opened the window and exclaimed to a somewhat startled policeman, "How nice that you are here!"

I explained my predicament and asked whether he could call for a breakdown van over his radio. The policeman was very helpful and did not even check whether I was sober or had a driving licence.

Fifteen minutes later a breakdown van appeared. The driver quickly lifted up the bonnet of my car, and soon we were on our way to the garage where I had had a booking for weeks. I marvelled at the fact that the police control point had appeared just there, just then, and thanked the universe for whatever it was that had arranged the whole thing so perfectly.

I never again saw any police at that place.

4 Are coincidences statistical or mystical?

Something unbelievable is waiting to become known.

Carl Sagan

Carl Jung was one of the great pioneers of and became an icon of psychology. He thought a lot about something he called "strange psychological parallel occurrences".

In his work as a psychotherapist he had noticed how sudden coincidences often became a turning point for his patients. Something happened at the same time both outside and inside the patient, an "aha" experience that started a healing process.

It was Jung who coined the term *synchronicity*. These events, he said, were not something that happened by blind chance but were *meaningful coincidences* – a sign of some kind of interplay between the psyche, matter, time and space. It was a long time before he dared to publish his thoughts and experiences of synchronicities. The whole idea was quite offensive to the scientific world.

But a well-known physicist, Wolfgang Pauli, was very interested in Jung's work. Pauli was a professor of theoretical physics and won a Nobel Prize in 1945. He had been an unusually gifted student who at just twenty-one won the admiration of Albert Einstein by virtue of a scientific paper about his theory of relativity. Einstein even called Pauli "my spiritual son". Pauli became one of the founders of the new quantum physics, together with Werner Heisenberg and Niels Bohr. It was also he who first proposed that there must exist a strange little particle he called the *neutrino*. Thirty years later scientists were able to verify that it did in fact exist. Nowadays many respectable scientists are searching for this little particle far out in space, as well as deep in the Earth. The flow of neutrinos is not stopped by a mere planet. During the few seconds it takes you to read this sentence, millions of neutrinos rush through your brain in their cosmic dance.

In the new physics they were facing phenomena that pulled the rug from under many of the longheld scientific beliefs about reality. When they penetrated the innermost parts of matter, they found that it did not just consist of smaller and smaller particles but of energy as well. The particles switched between being matter and energy, and irritatingly there was something about all this that could not be known or predicted. That was the basic premise of Heisenberg's famous "uncertainty principle". The most physical, materialistic and strict of all sciences had suddenly, to the chagrin of many, gone in for a bit of mysticism.

It was also discovered that what happened in an experiment was influenced by the person who undertook it. The observer influenced the observed. From there it was not such a big step to the question of the relationship between mind and matter. Perhaps this was the reason for Pauli's great interest in Jung's ideas. Synchronicity could be seen as an interplay between a person's inner state and what happens in the world outside. Between spirit and matter.

Pauli and Jung had intensive discussions about this, and

Pauli encouraged Jung to continue his work. In a letter to Pauli, Jung describes an event that has become something of a classic example of synchronicity. He is sitting with a rather difficult patient, a woman who seems stuck in her own beliefs. She will not let go of her very logical and rational worldview. Jung finds it hard to loosen up her rigid pose and begins to feel there is nothing more he can do to help her. He sees her as a hopeless case and thinks about terminating the therapy.

Then she tells him of a very vivid and clear dream she has had during the night. Somebody gives her an expensive piece of jewellery shaped as a golden scarab, a kind of beetle. At the very same moment the woman is describing her dream they hear a sound at the window. Something is bouncing against the glass as if trying to get in. Jung walks over to the window and opens it. A beetle, shimmering gold and green, flies into the room. It is a so-called "golden scarab", a *Cetonia aurata*. He catches it and hands it over to his patient with the words, "Here is your golden scarab."

The woman stares at the shimmering scarab and is visibly shaken. The incident begins to crack her strict worldview and she can finally let go of her rigidity. The therapy takes a whole new turn and leads to a successful result.

Was it a "pure coincidence"? In our ingrained worldview we tend to see time as a straight line. When something happens along that line there is always something before it on the line that caused it. We live with *causality*, the law of cause and effect, as a matter of course.

But quantum physics has discovered that in the world of elementary particles that is not always the case. An effect can suddenly happen that does not seem to have any cause. Sometimes an effect can even arise before a cause. The law of causality does not seem to be carved in stone. Is it totally unthinkable that it could be the same in the world of humans? Is it really impossible that things can happen without a visible, under-standable cause? Does there exist a kind of causal context on a different level from what we can see, measure and count?

This is of course unthinkable for anyone who is wedded to and comfortable with the old worldview, a worldview that definitively states that if something happens, no matter how strange, it is possible to mathematically calculate the statisti-cal probability and find a causal connection. There were, for instance, x number of scarabs, *Cetonia aurata*, in the area where Jung had his practice, even if, as he pointed out, they were fairly unusual. The probability that one of them should move into the geographical space and fly into the room where Jung and his patient are is y. The probability that it should occur at exactly the time when this special patient was sitting there is z. Thus there is nothing strange about a scarab flying into Jung's window. You simply perform a statistical calculation on x, y and z – it is pure mathematics.

But that is only a small and limited part of what really hap-pened. One calculates only that which can be calculated. One cannot include things such as meaningfulness in the equation. This will not be captured in any net of statistical models. What was the probability that the woman had just dreamt of a golden scarab? That it happened to be a so-called "golden scarab", of all possible insects, which knocked on the window at the very moment she was describing her dream? That at the time her therapy had stalled? That thanks to the incident she is able to move on and becomes as if reborn? Not only that: the golden scarab was an important symbol to the old Egyptians. It was the symbol for ... rebirth.

What was the probability that I would end up in the seat next to Gunnar Wessman, just as I had a great need to talk to him? It is probably possible to figure out some kind of statistical likelihood for the fact that he would sit in just that seat, on just that flight, to just that destination, on just that day. And also the probability that I unknowingly would get the seat right next to him. I have a great respect for mathematicians and statisticians, but how do you incorporate in a mathematical formula the fact that just then I had a great need to get together with and talk to Gunnar?

The statistical probability of Gunnar and I going to the same destination out of all possible destinations in the world, on the same day out of all possible days of the year, on the same flight out of all possible flights during that day, and ending up in the seats next to each other out of all possible seats in an aircraft, must be close to zero. The meaningfulness, on the other hand, was close to one.

Every truly synchronistic event has a strong element of *meaning* that cannot be calculated. The meaning is unique and specific to the person or persons involved. It does not exist on the material, mathematical level, but on the psychological, emotional level which statistics cannot reach or explain. No more than the number of letters on this page can explain anything about the content it communicates.

It is their very meaningfulness that makes certain coincidences break out of the constraints of statistics into the realm of synchronicity. This opens the door to other and much more interesting possibilities.

When I encountered Gunnar in the seat next to mine, I reacted peculiarly in two quite different ways. The intuitive part of my mind, which is often faster, thought, "Fine, I needed to talk to him, so here he is." The more logical, slower part, on the other hand, was quite taken aback. How on Earth did this happen? How strange. It was totally impossible to arrange a meeting, so how come we are suddenly sitting in a perfect meeting place without distractions?

That double way of reacting seems to be a pattern when synchronicity happens. The first immediate, emotional reaction is not wonderment but rather a kind of naturalness. Yes, perfect, I needed this, so it happened. Just as natural as the TV going on when I push the button.

But a fraction of a second later the intellect catches up and begins wondering and trying to interpret what has happened. How could this be? How strange. What luck I had!

Nowadays, though, my intellect has come to accept the synchronicities as something natural, even to expect them. It has stopped seeing them as something unnatural, but it has not stopped wondering.

Was there some sort of mystical connection between my intense desire in the world of thoughts and feelings, and what then happened in the physical world of time and space? Was it "just a coincidence" or was it something else? Does there in fact exist something in the universe beyond what we have been led to believe?

Perhaps there is a greater reality beyond the physical that we are so used to. And perhaps this greater reality, whatever it is, has an influence over the smaller reality that we are aware of through our senses.

Somebody said that statistics is like a bikini. It shows the obvious but hides the most interesting.

There is a lot that can be calculated with the help of mathematics and statistics. But hardly the meaning of a synchronistic event. That is more mystical, which does not mean that it is mysterious. It means only that we do not yet have enough knowledge, that it is something we cannot understand simply because we still lack this specific knowledge about it.

The most interesting.

5 The scarab and the grand piano

The piano tuner Tore Persson was tuning our grand piano in my study. I was sitting in the same room working on this book, but it was not very easy to concentrate on writing. Piano tuning is not particularly enjoyable as background music.

I stopped writing to leave the study and do something else. As I walked towards the door, Tore asked what I was working on, and I answered that I was trying to write a book.

"How interesting," he said. "What kind of a book?" I tried to explain that it was about something that the famous psychiatrist Carl Jung called *synchronicity*, which stood for *meaningful coincidence*. Tore looked puzzled.

I tried to explain by telling him Jung's story of the golden scarab (see Chapter 4). Since Jung himself had described the scarab incident as an example of synchronicity, why couldn't I? Tore found it interesting but soon resumed working on the piano while I left the study, carefully closing the door behind me.

I was about to host a jam session a few days later with some great professional musicians, such as the famous Strandberg brothers – Göran, who is a wizard at the piano, and trombone player Bertil, who, among his many credentials, played for four years with the legendary Artie Shaw Orchestra in the USA.

No wonder I was anxious to have the piano perfectly tuned. Getting to play with musicians like that was both a great challenge and a sublime experience for me. So even if I could not guarantee to always play perfectly in tune on my bass – it has no fixed playing positions – I at least wanted to contribute with a well-tuned piano. I could hear in the distance how Tore was getting along in there.

At the time I had some doubts about the book. How to handle such a vast and strange subject? Was I really capable of doing it? Would anyone want to read it? Should I continue to write, or maybe give up and just leave the half-finished manuscript in a drawer? Doubts swept like toxic banks of fog through my mind. It is said that writers are often struck with doubt while working on a new book. At the time I was struck pretty badly.

After about an hour the plinking in the study stopped. Tore appeared in the kitchen and said he had now finished with the grand. He accepted my offer of a cup of coffee and told me he had gone through the whole instrument. It was a good instrument, he said, but he had found two small foreign objects that had somehow ended up inside the mechanics of the piano. He held out his hand.

I looked. Then I stared.

In his hand were … a pen and a green scarab.

I am aware that you could simply say that someone had happened to drop a pen into the piano. Nothing strange about that. And the green scarab, obviously some sort of plastic toy, had probably ended up there with the help of my little daughter, who sometimes played in the study. It just happened. Nothing remarkable at all.

But to me the incident was most remarkable, loaded with meaning and strongly contributing to the fact that this book exists. *Aspect number 1*: Tore and I had just talked about synchronicity. *Aspect number 2*: I had just related to him the story of the green scarab as a symbol of synchronicity, of meaningful coincidence. *Aspect number 3*: I was wrestling with doubts about finishing this book about synchronicity. *Aspect number 4*: Of all the hundred thousand different things that could end up inside a grand piano, they were a pen, the symbol of writing, and a scarab, the symbol of synchronicity. *Aspect number 5*: Add to all that the statistically most probable fact that nothing had fallen into the piano.

I chose to interpret the incident as an extremely meaningful coincidence, a true example of synchronicity, not something that happened just by chance. I chose to interpret it as a nice way of telling me to keep up the writing.

6 Is now the time?

Every truth passes through three stages before it is
acknowledged.
First it is ridiculed.
Second it is opposed.
Third it is considered self-evident.

Arthur Schopenhauer

We know quite well what the world looked like to the
people of the sixteenth century. It is not the same world in
which we live. Earth was a big disc placed by God in the middle
of the universe, and on it he had created man as an image of
himself. Above the disc he had constructed the vault of heaven,
and in that he placed the sun, the moon and the stars, which he
slowly rotated, basically to please man. The earthly disc, *terra
firma*, was solid and still while the rest of the universe circled
around this absolute central point.

God was present in everything. In the trees and the stones,
in the weather and the crops, in diseases and fortunes. Everybody knew it was so. You knew because the priests said it
was so, and the priests knew. The priests were the highest

authority on the ways of the world. Religion was the ultimate truth.

Besides, you could experience it yourself through your senses. You did not feel the earth moving and spinning, and you could see with your own eyes that it was flat, even if there were mountains and valleys here and there. It was totally obvious and self-evident. It was the world view, the culture, the predominant paradigm.

But every culture contains the seeds of its own downfall and the beginning of something new. In Poland there was an astronomer, Copernicus, who had begun to feel that there was something wrong with the old world view. His studies of the heavens indicated that the Earth was not at all a fixed plate circled by the Sun. It seemed to be exactly the other way around. Copernicus realized that the Earth must instead be a sphere among other spheres that circled around the Sun and, besides, rotated about its own axis.

This was dynamite. These new ideas deeply offended the Church, and that was dangerous in the Europe of the Middle Ages. It had to be handled with the utmost care. But as Victor Hugo wrote: "Not even all the armies of the world can stop an idea whose time has come."

The German mathematician Johannes Kepler latched on to Copernicus's ideas and made calculations that showed that he was right. This was not well received. Another fresh thinker was the Italian Galileo Galilei, who constructed one of the world's first telescopes. The very first had been devised in Holland, but Galileo's was the biggest so far, and through it he could see that Copernicus and Kepler were right. It was the Earth and the Moon that circled the Sun, not the other way around. This became too much for the priests.

Galileo was close to being decapitated. The Church was

terribly upset over this blatant heresy. The Sun circles the Earth, period. Galileo offered the clergy the opportunity to come and see for themselves through his telescope. But they declined. There was no sense in doing that since they knew the facts. That is how defenders of the established world view usually react. Galileo was guilty of heresy, and in order to save his skin he was forced to publicly apologize. He had to state that Earth was a stationary disc circled by the Sun. But during the proceedings he is supposed to have whispered, "And yet she moves."

But no matter how the Church tried to stop it, the seed of a new world view had begun to grow. The French philosopher René Descartes gave it further nourishment. Through a series of dreams the idea had come to him that you could separate body and soul, spirit and matter. He said that they both existed together, but could also be viewed separately. That simple statement made it possible to study matter as something in itself without denying the existence of its spiritual connection.

This thought was not as violently offensive to the priesthood. They did not realize its explosive power, and no one could anticipate how far it would lead. But the snowball was now in full motion, and it grew further through Isaac Newton, the next midwife in the birth of the new world view. He formulated the natural laws and explained how the heavenly bodies were hurtling around each other. It is said that he discovered the law of gravity while sitting under an apple tree and being hit by a falling apple. Anyway, Newton's work became an important foundation for the emergence of all of Western industrialization.

Man began constructing machines and building companies, new sciences emerged and the world was changed for ever. The Earth was transformed from a stationary disc in the middle of the universe to a sphere among other spheres whirling around in the outskirts of a galaxy. And it was also rotating around its own axis. Diseases were no longer the work of God but of microorganisms. God also had to cede power over the weather and the crops to the laws of physics and biology.

Knowledge of reality moved away from religion and settled with science. Now it was the scientists, not the priests, who understood the ways of the world. The universe was seen as a big machine, and soon the scientists would be able to describe exactly how it functioned. Religious idealism was no longer king of the hill, done down by rational logic. Idealism changed into materialism.

A new era was born – an era that fundamentally changed man's way of seeing himself and his world, an era that has created fantastic things such as aeroplanes, computers and mobile phones. An era that has created greater prosperity for more people than ever before in the history of man, and totally changed our way of life. Humankind in the twenty-first century lives on a level that man in the sixteenth century had not even been able to fantasize about.

But nothing lasts for ever.

Now, at the beginning of a new millennium, we are beginning to notice that this fantastic existence also has its shadowy side. There are more and more people on Earth, and at the same time thousands of other life forms, plants and animals, are disappearing forever because of the actions of humans. Allergies are increasing almost epidemically. It is no longer just the laws of physics that influence the climate, but humankind itself.

Our total body of knowledge is increasing exponentially. Ninety per cent of all scientists who have ever lived on Earth are active today. We know infinitely more than they did in the sixteenth century, but have we become wiser?

We have more and more advanced medicines, but are we healthier?

We have much better housing, but do we have better homes?

The police have increasingly more sophisticated methods at their disposal, but are we safer?

We have ever more electrical machines and electronic gadgets to save time and work for us, but are we less stressed?

Something is not quite right. Why are so many young people committing suicide? Why are more and more people stressed and burnt out? Where does all the unprovoked violence come from, and why is there so little unprovoked kindness? Why are the environmental problems growing in spite of the fact that we know what causes them and where they lead? We have infinitely more possessions today, but are we happier?

The old religious superstition has been exchanged for a materialistic rationality. Perhaps it will turn out that materialism is actually just a new form of superstition. Perhaps the problems of our time are a sign that our world view is once again about to crack. Perhaps the materialistic era is fast running out of possibilities.

Perhaps we are once again standing on the threshold of a new era, just as they did in the sixteenth century. Perhaps the seed of something new has once again begun to germinate. If so, what is the new era all about?

Nobody knows for sure, but I think that an important part of the new world view will be an upgrade of human consciousness. Leading-edge science today indicates that human consciousness might turn out to be something much more and much stranger than we have been led to believe. Something that cannot be explained just in terms of ganglia, synapses, chemicals and electromagnetic impulses in the brain.

Materialism has dominated science and research. Two concepts that have been especially important are *positivism* and *reductionism*. Positivism has nothing to do with positive thinking; it means that only that which can be measured, weighed and calculated exists. That which cannot be proven, weighed and measured, or repeatedly experimented on, is disregarded.

It has often been a wise strategy that has kept science on a strict and credible level, has created great knowledge and useful machines such as microwave ovens and dialysis apparatus. But at the same time it has been incapable of providing us with answers to our deeper questions. It does not say much about the nature of our consciousness. How are we able to think? How are we able to experience? How are we able to remember? Those questions have until now been largely disregarded by science.

Reductionism means that to gain knowledge about something you reduce it to its smallest parts, which you then study more closely. By analysing the molecules of a car tyre, for example, you could gain some knowledge about the properties of the tyre.

But that works only partially. A whole is always more than the sum of its parts. The human brain is something more than the sum of its molecules. A melody is something more than the sum of its notes. You cannot experience a poem by Keats by studying the chemistry of the printer's ink. You cannot find Mozart by taking apart your stereo. You cannot understand a Rembrandt by analysing the molecules of the paint. Our inner experiences do not only have to do with atoms and molecules. Yet they are very real.

I believe that we are in that dizzying moment when a circus performer has let go of one trapeze but has not yet grasped the next. Watch carefully and you will see that the next trapeze is on its way, even if the grand performance we are part of today, the changing of world views, is in slow motion. I believe that the new world view, or paradigm, will develop slowly, like a photo in the developing tray. But it will lead to an even more dramatic and strange shift in our heads than that which happened when the Earth was transformed from a stationary disc to a whirling sphere. Then the transformation took about a hundred and fifty years. In our time it will be faster.

When Vaclav Havel was awarded the Philadelphia Liberty Medal in 1994, he said in a speech:

I believe there are good reasons to consider the modern era as finished. Today there is so much that indicates that we are in a state of transformation, where something seems to be on its way out and something else is painfully being born. It is as if something was about to disintegrate, rot, putting an end to itself, while something else, still undefined, is about to rise up from the debris.

Something is definitely happening. Scientific efforts to study consciousness and the brain are increasing dramatically. The human brain is, possibly alongside the deepest parts of the sea, the last continent on Earth that has not yet been fully investigated. Perhaps we will soon realize that human consciousness is the most central and important thing of all. That it is infinitely more than just a collection of measurable processes inside our skulls. And that there is a hitherto unknown link between mind and matter – a link that may not necessarily be a prisoner even within the barriers of time and space.

In the old materialistic world view, man is a physical construction that has somehow happened to develop a consciousness, and eventually we will be able to map and describe exactly how and why it works. It is basically just a matter of chemical reactions and electrochemical impulses in the brain.

But what if it is discovered that the exact opposite is the case? What if it turns out that we are not a physical apparatus that has developed a consciousness, but a consciousness that has developed a physical apparatus.

This might well be a part of the new world view, even if it is as hard for some people to accept as it was for the priests of Rome to accept that the Earth is a whirling sphere.

7 Old boats

The sea was glittering between the tree trunks at the summer residence of the Frisk family. The newly caught and prepared Baltic herring was delicious, and perfectly cooled beverages enveloped us in that special atmosphere which can only be experienced on a mild summer evening in the Stockholm archipelago. The perfect start to a long sailing vacation.

The conversation flowed between deep questions and giggly nonsense. I came to think of our old sailing boat, *Mantra*, an English Westerly 28, which we had sold some years earlier to a family named Bertenstam. It was a very quick deal in spite of the fact that I was not quite sure I really wanted to sell it.

I had put an ad in the paper, mostly to feel my way. But already at eight in the morning the phone was ringing. It was Bertenstam, my first potential buyer. He wanted to come immediately and have a look at the boat.

He showed up an hour later. My ambivalence made me very honest about the various imperfections of the boat. There was a strange noise in the engine, the radio antenna was broken, and so on. To my surprise Bertenstam grew more and more enthusiastic the more faults I revealed. Finally he was totally enchanted and absolutely wanted to buy the boat. No fuss, no bargaining – he wanted it, period. His enthusiasm blew away my wishy-washy feelings, and before I knew it the deal was done.

Later I understood that Bertenstam just loved to busy himself with repairing stuff. He had grown up in a motor shop, he said, and engines were a lot of fun. Had the boat been in perfect condition there would have been no deal.

Some years had passed, and I wondered where he was now. Did he still own *Mantra*? Was he still satisfied? Nobody knew.

The next morning we set sail and glided idly away in a light breeze and wonderful sunny weather. We anchored for lunch in a small island inlet, and then sailed onward to ... to where? Where should we cast anchor for the night? We had no specific route planned but had decided to sail wherever the winds would blow us. This day they blew us to the Lökholmen island close to Sandhamn, the eastern-most little port in the archipelago. Towards evening we glided slowly into the Lökholmen inlet.

It was crowded. Lots of boats had anchored side by side with their noses facing the solid rock sloping towards the waterline. It seemed too tight for one more, so I thought we would have to spend the night swinging at anchor in the bay. But as I scanned the row of boats I thought I detected a narrow gap between two of them. It might be just wide enough for us to squeeze into. After various manoeuvres we succeeded, with two mooring ropes ashore, the anchor holding the rear and a row of fenders between us and the neighbouring boats. It was tight, but that is usually accepted in the middle of the summer when everybody is out in the archipelago.

After the rather stressful business of mooring there is always a pleasant feeling of relaxation. You take a breather in the cockpit, perhaps with a shot of whisky at hand, checking up on the surroundings and enjoying life for a moment.

I suddenly thought there was something familiar about the boat to our left. Isn't that … it seems to be … yes, it *is* our old boat *Mantra*!

At that very moment, Bertenstam popped up in the cockpit.

Oh yes, he was still sailing the old *Mantra*, which was now in absolute top condition. And he was still pleased with her. We spent a pleasant evening together, and all my questions from the previous evening were answered.

There was just one unanswered question though. On a sunny day in July there are about two hundred thousand boats among the 24,000 islands in that vast area that is the Stockholm archipelago. How come we ended up side by side with just that one boat we had thought about only the night before?

8 Is there a doctor out here?

The next morning we bid farewell to Bertenstam and sailed north. The south-westerly wind began to abate towards midday, but the sun was shining and we were in no hurry, having no particular goal, just enjoying the beauty of it all. In the afternoon we were in a total lull close to the island group of Rödlöga. Suddenly a strong wind blew up from the north. OK, then, let's go to Rödlöga for the night. There is a small country shop there where we can replenish our supplies.

But the northerly wind increased steadily and made it less practical to anchor at the main island. Instead we chose the smaller island just across the strait to the north, where we would be sheltered from the wind which was now getting pretty angry. We were almost alone there except for two boats that had anchored a hundred metres to our right. Some boat people prefer to be a bit secluded if possible, while others prefer the togetherness of being side by side. I belong to those who would rather have a bit of space between me and the next boat.

Just as we were tidying up the boat after the morning's sailing I heard a sharp bang and a strange sound from the stern. I called for Agneta, my wife at the time, but got no answer, just a whining. I rushed down into the forepeak and found her lying on a couch with one hand holding the other. What had happened? She showed me her hand, where a nasty gash had opened across a finger. The hatch to the forepeak had slammed shut in the wind while she still had her hand on the rim. It was a deep gash, and the crazy association occurred to me of a tomato having fallen to the floor and cracked.

We did have a first-aid kit on board and I tried to fix the gash with some surgical tape, but I realized that it had to be stitched. By whom? My thoughts were racing. Was there a doctor on the main island? Who would know?

I must get to the shop, they'll know. And there is a telephone. But how do I get there? It is at least a hundred metres across the strait and we have no dinghy.

I told Agneta to stay calm and just lay there and rest, I would get a doctor. I jumped ashore and ran to one of the other boats that I saw had a dinghy. I explained the situation and asked whether I could borrow it. Sure, go ahead. I got into the dinghy and started rowing frantically across the strait.

Then a thought hit me. Is there someone or something up there that can help us? If so, please do so. I directed my plea to the heavy grey clouds without really expecting an answer. I could not hang on to the thought, as I had to focus on handling the little dinghy in the choppy water.

But the next moment another thought popped up. I realized that I needed coins in order to use the public telephone at the shop. This was before mobile phones had changed our lives. I quickly turned the dinghy around and rowed towards our boat to pick up some money.

Just as I approached our boat I saw that another sailing boat had come in and anchored very close to our left. An unknown man stood on deck, handling a rope, and suddenly it was as if I heard a voice just behind me, slightly above my head and to the right. "He is a doctor."

In my upset condition I did not react normally. Instead of being surprised and turning to see where the voice had come from, I just thought, Oh, good, and heard myself saying to the man with the rope: "Excuse me, but my wife has just had an accident, and since you are a doctor, could you come over and help her?"

He dropped the rope, looked at me, astonished, and asked: "How did you know I am a doctor?"

I suddenly realized the oddity of the situation. What could I say? I did not succeed in giving him a satisfactory answer, but mumbled something about just taking a chance. I did not dare say that I somehow thought I heard a voice from space or wherever it came from.

He went down into his cabin, came up with a doctor's bag and came on board our boat. While he attended to Agneta's injury he asked several times: "We have never met; how did you know I am a doctor?"

I still have no answer to that question.

9 *The double bass and the therapist*

I tried to get some kind of meaningful notes out of my new German double bass. I realized more and more what a cumbersome and difficult instrument it is. But I enjoyed the fact that real notes actually emerged when I plucked the strings, and that it sounded just like a double bass is supposed to sound.

That had not been the case with my first bass, a small, cheap school bass made of plywood. When I bought it I knew nothing about the double bass, only that I wanted to learn how to play it. The whole idea with an instrument is that it should emit notes, but this one had got it all wrong. It sucked in the notes instead. When you plucked a string all you heard was a short, dull "poff" and then silence. I did have some idea of how a double bass should sound, and I thought that the total unwillingness of this instrument to produce any kind of viable notes must be due to my glaring inability.

One day it happened to crash to the floor, and when I picked it up the whole fingerboard was hanging loose in the strings. It had broken right off. Who could fix something like that? I had no idea, but got a tip from the journalist Oscar Hedlund. "Talk to George," he said, "George Bohlin. He can fix just about any instrument. Tell him I sent you."

I was sceptical. George Bohlin, the world famous instrument

maker, who had built the grand piano that Bill Evans had been so enchanted by. The one Evans had played on the famous recording with Monica Zetterlund. Surely I could not go to the great George Bohlin with such a trifling matter as this.

"George isn't like that. He is a good guy. Just say I sent you," said Oscar. And so it happened that the famous instrument maker actually repaired my worthless little school bass. He did a formidable job. When I came to pick it up it was in much better shape than when I had left it. The repair where the fingerboard had snapped was totally invisible. I realized that I would have to pay a lot more for this job than I had originally paid for the bass itself. Such exquisite workmanship must cost.

"No, it doesn't cost anything," said George.

I didn't understand. "But you must have spent a lot of time doing such a fine job."

"No, I don't want to charge any money for this."

I felt stupid and kept insisting.

"No," George said. "My master taught me an important thing. He said, Don't charge anything for trifles. For big things you charge big, but not for trifles. And this was a trifle."

My protests were to no avail. His mind was made up and all I could do was to thank him and express my appreciation.

"But I have to tell you one thing," he said, and gave me a serious look. "This is not a good instrument."

That didn't bother me as much as he might have thought. It somehow felt good to hear it from this expert, because then I could tell myself that the lousy sound was not only due my incompetence.

The short meeting with George Bohlin taught me something. First, not to charge for trifles, and second, if you have agreed to do a job, even if it is a trifle, you do the best you can.

The hopeless little bass was now elegantly repaired, but

still refused to offer any decent sound. Not even George Bohlin had been able to change that.

Since I was still anxious to produce some kind of bass notes at our sporadic jam sessions, I bought an electric bass instead. The little double bass got a vacation and I thought of trying to sell it. But my wife at the time, Agneta, thought it looked nice and wanted to have it standing in a corner as a decoration. She still has it.

The electric bass certainly produced a lot of sound, but eventually I got tired of that too. No matter how much I adjusted the various buttons on the instrument and the amplifier, it still sounded too electric. I never succeeded in getting that wooden double-bass sound that I longed for. That would be possible only with a real, old double bass. But where do you find one like that? I had no idea; I knew only that you are unlikely to find one in an ordinary music store.

I had just learnt that the finest double basses in the world were made before the First World War. The master craftsmen gathered wood high up in the European mountains where spruce and maple grew slowly and achieved the right density. Then it was stored for a long time to dry and achieve just the right quality and structure before it was moulded into instruments.

But many of the master craftsmen's workshops were situated in those parts of Europe where the First World War was fought for years – miles of muddy trenches where soldiers froze, starved and died during this endless hell. To save their lives, cook food and stay warm they took what they could find in the way of wood and other flammable stuff.

That was the end of the instrument makers' fine, stored mountain wood. Since then the stocks have never recovered. Times changed and it became too expensive and cumbersome to bring the wood down from the mountains. The handling of wood and the making of instruments became less of a handcraft and more industrialized. That is why the best double basses were made before the First World War.

I hoped to find such an oldie. That was one of two intentions or desires that occupied me daily. The other was to find a good therapist.

By this time our marriage had hit some turbulence. We had tried two different varieties of therapy to get help, but with rather meagre results. One was with a therapist couple in whom neither of us had any confidence. The other was with a psychiatrist, a peculiar and mean man whom neither of us liked either. The therapy ended after a couple of sessions, when I, in an angry mood, told him that if there was anyone in this room who needed therapy it was he.

I realized that in the world of psychotherapy, just as in any other world, there is a great difference between good and bad. There are good and bad dentists, good and bad lawyers, good and bad advertising people; the problem is to see and understand the difference when you yourself are not inside that world.

A synchronistic vortex began influencing things. Two wholly separate events happened almost simultaneously, and got intertwined in a way that elegantly solved both of my problems.

The first was my jazz pal Dick Nilson telling me that he had heard of a person who had an old double bass for sale. His name was Sven Söderberg. I contacted him and we set a time for me to come and look at his bass.

The other was that I got a call from a lady who had read an interview with me in a magazine, and she asked whether my agency could possibly help her with a special project she was working on. She presented herself as Monica Getz, and we set a time for a meeting at my office.

I visited Söderberg, a nice man who had been both a jazz musician and a sea captain. Now he wanted to sell his German double bass from the nineteenth century. I eagerly fingered the strings and was elated by the fact that this instrument actually produced real bass notes. Besides, it felt easy to play, so I was close to making a deal.

While we talked jazz and bass playing, Sven happened to mention that he was a second-year student of psychotherapy at the Gestalt Academy. I was startled. He must know the therapy world! I took a chance and described our search. Could he maybe recommend someone?

He understood and said that the best option of all was a therapist named Lars Norberg, who also happened to be the principal of the Gestalt Academy. But to get him was impossible, he was much too busy. Anyway, Sven promised to give it some thought and come back to me with some names. It was at least a beginning.

When Monica Getz came to the office and handed over her business card, I could not help but ask about her surname. Was she possibly related to Stan Getz, a legend, one of the greatest tenor saxophone players in the history of jazz? Oh yes, she had been married to Stan, but they were now divorced. She did not appear too eager to talk about the matter any further. Her errand was about something quite different, a new method for treating alcoholics. It was called the Hazelden Method or the Minnesota Model, and she was about to introduce it in Sweden, together with the chief physician of Scandinavian Airlines. They would start off with a big conference at the Grand Hotel. Could we help them with the publicity? They had very little money.

Maybe it was because she had been married to Stan Getz

that I said yes, and even that we would do it as a so-called "pro bono project", meaning that we would not charge anything. She was very pleased and offered in return to come to the agency with the SAS doctor one evening to show a video about the Hazelden Method, and inform the staff of the various faces of alcoholism and its warning signs. Since, statistically, one out of every ten people have a predisposition to alcoholism, it was reasonable to assume that in our company a number of people would be in the danger zone. I accepted her offer and we arranged an evening for the event.

When Sven and I met again to close the bass deal, I could not resist telling him about my meeting with the ex-wife of Stan Getz. I also mentioned her errand. Sven's eyebrows went up. He became visibly engaged.

"That sounds very interesting. The fact is that I am actually on my way to specializing in addiction therapy. Is there a chance that I could come and listen to that presentation?" Sure, he was welcome.

A few days later Sven called.

"I just talked to Lars Norberg. He is also very interested in the Hazelden Method and wanted me to ask you whether he could come as well to that evening at your office.

"But of course!" I was very eager to meet the famous therapist, and now a chance had popped up from nowhere.

The evening turned out to be very informative and interesting, but to me the most interesting aspect was meeting Lars Norberg. The great therapist proved to be not at all as distant and difficult to reach as I had imagined. On the contrary, he was a very sympathetic man with lots of warmth, and I of course took the chance to ask him whether there was a possibility that he would see me and my wife. To my surprise he said yes without hesitation.

There is nowadays quite a bit of talk about "the law of attraction" and "the power of intention". The idea being that if you hold something firmly in mind, a desire or need, that mental and emotional focus will attract solutions.

I don't know. I had never heard of these things at the time, but I was pretty preoccupied with the two desires, finding a good double bass and a good therapist. Within two weeks this little synchronistic vortex had produced both – a good bass of just the right age, and the best possible therapist.

Norberg guided us to a decent divorce, if there is such a thing. At least he helped us avoid the usual pitfalls and part as friends.

10 *The apartment*

We were in the middle of our separation, and I needed to rent an apartment short term where I could live for a while and contemplate the situation. A small two-room furnished flat would be ideal. But where could I find one like that?

I had not looked for a place to live for more than twenty years, and had only a vague notion that it might not be so easy. The newspaper ads had nothing to offer and the local housing authority probably did not bother with such temporary solutions. Besides, there would most likely be a five-year waiting list through the official channels. That is usually the case when the government is supposed to handle the distribution of something that many people want – as in East Germany, where you supposedly had to wait fifteen years for a Trabant car.

I had to find another solution, and seemed to remember having seen a small sign about apartments in a window on the street just around the corner from the office. Was it still there? I went down and found it, slightly askew, but still hanging there. As my need was acute, I went in.

A man in his thirties sat behind a large desk. The furniture had no significant attributes and the atmosphere was not noticeably welcoming. Someone from the tax authorities would probably experience it as distinctly unfriendly. But I needed a flat urgently so I pushed my slight apprehension aside.

The man gave me a suspicious look when I began to describe my requirements. Gradually he understood that I did not have any agenda other than what I said. He thawed slightly. Sure, he would probably be able to find something for me. His fee would be a couple of thousand and a hundred in hand right away to start looking. OK. I gave him a hundred and felt quite hopeful as I came back out into the blinding autumn sunlight on the street.

Maybe I had exaggerated the difficulties, maybe it was no more complicated than this, I thought, as I climbed the stairs to the office. He did seem like a shifty type, but as long as he gets me an apartment quickly, no matter. All I have to do is make sure that I, or someone else, does not get screwed.

Back in my office I tried to focus on the usual river of daily concerns, but my thoughts lingered on the rather limited cosiness of the apartment broker's office. Other thoughts began to squeeze into my mind. Muddy feelings of guilt about the separation. Did we do the right thing? Was everything my fault? Was it stupid to get an apartment in the city? Did the whole thing become more definite that way? My thoughts rumbled on but were abruptly stopped by the telephone ringing.

"Hi, this is Bengt."

Bengt Stern was a good friend who as a medical doctor never hesitated to challenge the medical establishment. He often thought and acted at the absolute leading edge of healing practice, which had caused the medical authorities to cast an ominous eye on his place in the medical register. Against many odds he had started the Mullingstorp Health and Education Centre, and made it into one of the world's most effective places for personal development. Eventually, even the medical authorities had begun sending patients to Mullingstorp. A decent revenge for Bengt.

"Hi, Bengt, how are you?"

"Great, thank you. I just called to ask you about something. You see, I have a newly restored and furnished two-room apartment on Bastugatan with a beautiful sea view. I want to let it for a year and I just thought that you might know someone who would be interested."

That I did.

The odd synchronicity made me feel that this must be the right thing to do. I signed up directly without hesitation and without even having seen it. Directly after the phone conversation with Bengt, I called the apartment guy and said that he could skip the search and keep the hundred.

The apartment turned out to be just as nice as Bengt had described it. The furniture, on the other hand, would hardly inspire a feature in *Beautiful Homes*. It was even actively ugly. Each time I entered the apartment the ugliness came alive and threw itself at me. The furniture had previously done its job in some old doctor's office, and now it had obviously been retired to the flat, awaiting the executioner's axe.

But I liked that ugliness. It was part of my punishment. It served me right. It dampened my feelings of guilt a wee bit, but as soon as I looked out of the window they returned with full force. The view over the water was just a bit too beautiful.

11 What is it we are a part of?

Our knowledge is but a drop in the ocean of ignorance.

William James

What science knows about reality is just a fraction of what there is to know. That is an insight that should lead to some measure of humbleness. Nobody can explain the energy that is pulsating in your arteries, nobody can explain how you can have a consciousness, nobody can explain how you can develop from just a glimmer in your father's eye.

What is it that we don't know? The horizon of human knowledge is pushed farther and farther out. We conquer the unknown piece by piece, yet we are only a small distance from the shore of the enormous ocean of ignorance. What secrets are hiding out there beyond the horizon?

What is this strange episode we experience between the cradle and the grave? What is it we call life? How is it possible that a little seed from a birch tree contains the promise of a thousand forests?

We know that matter consists of molecules which in turn consist of atoms which in turn consist of elementary particles and so on. But where does it all come from? How did it all begin? How have these atoms been able to organize themselves into something as incredibly awesome as a human being? And why? There must be some kind of intention involved, some sort of intelligence that influences what happens in the material world.

One single cell in a human body is more complicated than the most advanced computer, and we have many trillions of cells, all with their various specialities. One produces chemicals in the brain, one kills bacteria, one cleans the blood, and so on. How is it possible? How could this fantastic, unimaginable apparatus that is the human body emerge from some molecules in the foam on a beach? Regardless of how many bolts of lightning struck, if that is indeed what happened.

Not only that. Even if dead matter in some miraculous way should have succeeded in organizing itself into the living vehicle that is the material human body, how did it manage to create a driver too – what we call our consciousness? How can something as non-material as consciousness arise from something as non-conscious as matter?

Some may sneer at such questions. It is almost foolish to ask since there are no answers anyway. Others believe that they have the answer and say there is nothing strange about it at all. Darwin has explained everything once and for all. A bit of foam on a beach of an ancient sea, lightning strikes, a chemical reaction takes place, and – hey presto! – evolution begins. And now, some billions of years later, we walk around as the crowning achievement of creation. Living proof of the theory of "survival of the fittest". Nothing strange about that.

Well, I find it extremely strange. Some dead matter on that beach got an electric shock and eventually there was a Jesus, a Socrates, a Shakespeare and an Einstein.

In 1981 the astronomers Chandra Wickramasinghe and Fred Hoyle mathematically calculated the likelihood that human beings had arisen that way. They found that the probability was the same as that of a hurricane in a scrapyard happening to assemble a jumbo jet.

The German professor Werner Gitt has conducted an interesting study of human DNA. He calculated how much information there is in a small lump of DNA as big as the head of a pin. If you wrote down all that information in a series of pocket books and put them in a pile on top of each other, how high would it be? Werner Gitt found that it would be equivalent to 500 piles of books reaching from the Earth to the Moon.

How in the world is it possible to transfer such an enormous quantity of information from one generation to the next? There is apparently no scientific law that can explain how life of such dignity could have emerged from dead matter.

Behind all this complicated information, must there not be an intelligent sender? Some form of consciousness?

All credit to Darwin, but his teaching is hardly the whole truth. It is very likely that the giraffe has achieved his long neck because those individuals with the longest necks were those that could best reach the food high up in the trees. They survived more easily, grew stronger and were therefore more attractive on the mating market. Thus it was their hereditary disposition for long necks that dominated and strengthened through the millennia.

It is a totally plausible explanation, but I am still not satisfied. There must be another story too. I am not thinking of some biblical childhood story where a bearded old man sits in his Heaven looking down on Earth, calling out in a thunderous voice, "Let there be life!" There must be a truth beyond that, a story for our time, even if it is not yet fully written.

I believe that the new story will be about a non-material reality, a field of intelligence, consciousness, information and energy that exists always and everywhere independent of time and space. A field that will prove to be the greater reality beyond the smaller reality that we can see and touch.

Our personal little consciousness is part of that greater consciousness, although we are not conscious of it. Just as a cell in my big toe is probably not conscious of being part of a greater whole, namely me. But I, being that greater whole, am aware of the existence of that cell. On the other hand I don't know much about the greater whole that I myself am probably a part of. I cannot know, but I can believe.

E. F. Schumacher has given the unknown an elegant angle. He mentions four levels or realms on Earth: mineral, plant, animal and human, and says that each level contains the lower levels but also something more, something higher, something unknown.

The lowest level, mineral or matter, that which we can weigh and measure, he gives the denomination M. It is a part of the next level, the plant world. Plants thus contain M but also something more that we cannot weigh or measure; that which we call life. Plants live and procreate. Since we do not quite know what life is, it becomes an X factor. The plant world is thus M+X.

The next level, the animal world, contains that which exists on the two lower levels, M+X, but also a new unknown factor, namely a form of consciousness. It exists as the ant's instinct to carry a pine needle home to its stack, the wish of the swallow to fly south in the autumn; it exists in our dog, Silly, jumping for joy when she understands that it is time for a walk. The inexplicable consciousness of the animal world is a Y factor, and we now have two unknowns: M+X+Y.

The highest realm we know about, that of us human beings, contains M and X and Y, but we have a further unknown aspect, another level of consciousness. We are conscious of being conscious. We can think forwards and backwards in time, we can plan, we know that we are going to die, we can contemplate the meaning of life and what to eat for dinner tonight. Human beings thus contain matter, M, but also no less than three levels of something unknown; life, consciousness and the ability to reflect. We then become $M+X+Y+Z$.

The plot thickens. M is all that we can weigh and measure. The rest is in the non-material realm. And still, that may be just a small fraction, the only fraction we know about, of a much greater spectrum. Our ears can hear sounds only within a very limited frequency span, and our eyes can see only within a certain span of light frequencies. With the help of instruments we can reach a little farther, to ultraviolet, infrared, and then some. But what is there beyond that?

Science has been fairly successful in penetrating M, matter. Aided by instruments, it can see that M consists of molecules that in turn consist of atoms, and beyond them the quantum physicists keep looking for elementary particles – quarks, leptons, bosons, neutrinos and other exotic minuteness. But these elusive entities seem to switch between being at times particles and at others energy in a chaotic cloud of possibilities. There, somewhere, is the horizon of human knowledge.

At the other end of this spectrum there is consciousness, which only lately has become subject of more extensive studies. Why should not the progression of levels continue in that direction too? Why could there not exist even higher levels of consciousness containing the lower levels of X, Y and Z, but also something beyond that?

Could it be that when we die we just let go of the lowest,

heaviest and densest level, M, matter, the body, and then go on with the others intact?

Could it be that the non-material part of us then unites with the greater field of consciousness?

Throughout human history people have intuitively believed in something higher they call God or Allah or the Unified Field or the Quantum Hologram or a number of other names. One of the more advanced descriptions I have heard is "a non-local field of energy and information with cybernetic, self-referral individual feedback loops". It probably does not matter what we call it – God, the Field or Steven. It is there anyway, as a cosmic intelligence far beyond our comprehension. To me that is the only plausible explanation for the mystery. A kind of spiritual internet that we are all connected to via our own inner personal computer. We are constantly influenced by it, and it is constantly influenced by us, by our thoughts, feelings and intentions. It is a very interactive situation.

Man has always had ideas about higher powers that have varied through the millennia. The Vikings had Oden, Thor and the whole gathering at Valhalla. The ancient Greeks had Zeus and all his gods at Olympus. The Hindu world abounds with gods around Krishna, the Muslims have Allah; the Christians are also content with just one spiritual authority, God, but at least he has Jesus, Mary and a lot of saints and angels around him. The shamanistic religions live with a plethora of different spirits and deities. The atheists of our time, who refuse to acknowledge any deities at all, are a comparatively small minority in the world. And after all, their notion that there is nothing that could be called God is itself a belief, a faith.

It seems that most people do have an innate need to believe in something greater than themselves. Maybe it is not just a belief, after all.

Many people through the millennia have actually experienced a connection with something higher, something indescribable, something beyond the material world. They have experienced "the Field" in different ways, and then tried to interpret the experience into something that the daily consciousness can grasp.

There are millions of such stories throughout human history. Some of them, such as the experiences of Jesus, Buddha and Mohammed, have even given birth to new religions.

There are also numerous attempts in literature and poetry to describe the experience of contact with this higher reality. But everyone that has experienced it seems to agree that it cannot be described in a common way. Words such as "light", "love", "wholeness", "ecstasy" and "feeling" are considered faint and inadequate echoes of what has been experienced. The language is prisoner within the walls of time and space, but the Field is beyond the walls and therefore language cannot adequately describe it.

There are many simpler and more commonplace things which are as impossible to describe. I would not be able to describe to you what a strawberry tastes like. If you had never tasted a strawberry, the only way for you to find out what it was like would be to eat one yourself.

Perhaps Lao Tse, the father of Taoism, best formulated the difficulty in communicating the experience of wholeness. When asked "What is Tao?", he replied: "He who knows does not speak. He who speaks does not know."

12 *Gustaf and Kim*

Kim von Platen is the son of the late, legendary newspaper man Gustaf von Platen. Father and son did not have much contact and lived their lives pretty much each to himself. Gustaf was the editor-in-chief of *Svenska Dagbladet*, one of the main Swedish daily newspapers, and Kim was one of the leaders at the advertising agency Söderqvist & Platen.

"Kim and I have always lived far apart and never really had a close relation, which I regret," said Gustaf. "We are probably both a little sad about the fact that we don't see each other very often."

Kim felt the same. "We are close in a way and have great respect for each other, but it is like some kind of hate-love. We almost never get together."

Father and son did harbour the same deep inner desire for closer contact, but something in their outer behaviour prevented it from happening. Could these deep, but unrealized, emotions have something to do with what was actually about to happen? Gustaf thought so.

Kim was on a golf tour in England together with his wife and her parents. His father-in-law was a well-known horse expert and radio personality. It happened to be a time of parliamentary elections in Great Britain, the ones in which Margaret

Thatcher was elected prime minister. Kim and company found themselves that evening in Trafalgar Square, where the Londoners traditionally gather on election nights to follow the final count of votes on large screens.

The crowded square was full of life. More than ten thousand people commented, laughed, mumbled and bickered while the figures flashed on the big screens. The atmosphere was jolly.

Suddenly Kim felt that there was something familiar about the man standing immediately to his right. It was his father, Gustaf.

Gustaf was in London to cover the election on behalf of his newspaper, *Svenska Dagbladet*. He had asked the managing editor what Londoners usually did when there was an election, and was told that they always gathered at Trafalgar Square – that was the place to be. In the evening Gustaf went there with his photographer to catch the excitement and the atmosphere.

In the crowd he suddenly thought he heard Swedish being spoken and looked around. There, right next to him, was his son Kim. They discovered each other simultaneously. Neither of them knew that the other was in London. The evening ended with a dinner at Rules.

A few years later Kim was on a company trip to Paris with his advertising agency. He knew that his father was stationed there as a correspondent at the time, but he had not wanted to contact him since the agency had a pretty tight schedule, and Kim felt a responsibility as leader of the group. Time simply would not allow for a visit to his father.

They checked in at the hotel. Kim, who likes photography, wanted to take the opportunity to get a few quick pictures before lunch, so he took a walk together with a colleague from the agency. They walked towards the Place de la Concorde and had a cup of coffee at a café before they walked out on to the large open space. Kim wanted to get some shots of the big Egyptian obelisk from Luxor presiding in the middle of the square. Place de la Concorde is the largest open space in Paris, and it was there that Louis XVI, Marie Antoinette and Robespierre, and many others, were beheaded.

The big square was, as is often the case, almost empty. Parisians seldom walk there – it is mostly the occasional tourist who challenges the eternal merry-go-round of cars at the periphery. Kim and his friend started to photograph the magnificent obelisk. They hardly noticed a single person approaching from far away, a small dot that gradually assumed human form. The wanderer's trajectory would take him straight to the point where Kim stood. As he got closer Kim thought there was something familiar about the figure. It soon proved to be a very familiar figure, namely his father, Gustaf von Platen.

"I got the idea that I should walk via Place de la Concorde. There are a thousand ways to get to where I was going, I was to do an interview with President Pompidou, but for some reason I felt that today I should take this route straight across the open space," said Gustaf.

When he got closer to the monument he noticed two people taking photographs. One of them seemed somehow familiar, and he soon saw that it was his son, Kim. He had no idea that Kim was in Paris. Considering how big Paris is and how many people swarm about the city on any given day, the probability that they would meet was not very great. The meeting resulted once again in a dinner together.

A few years later Gustaf was on a trip to New York to do a story for his newspaper. He had a few hours free, so just wandered the streets, which is such a nice thing to do in Manhattan. He found himself at the big department store Bloomingdale's on Third Avenue, and decided to go in. Once inside he continued to stroll around with no particular goal, amazed at the enormous display of wares. He stopped a bit absent-mindedly at a revolving display of ties.

Kim did not know that Gustaf was in New York. He had gone there with his business partner Stig Söderqvist. One of their clients was the telephone company Telia, and they were there to visit the big advertising agency N. W. Ayers, which worked with Telias's counterpart in the USA, AT&T.

In the little agency Söderqvist & Platen there were just thirteen people. At N. W. Ayers there were over six hundred working exclusively with AT&T.

Stig and Kim presented a campaign they had run for Telia in Sweden. The Ayers people liked it a lot and asked whether they could use the same campaign theme. Sure, why not, and the Söderqvist & Platen concept was published all over the USA. But they never received any remuneration.

Stig tells of how he suddenly saw Kim and Gustaf standing on opposite sides of a tie display. Kim tried to rotate it to see more of the ties, but he felt there was some resistance.

"I wondered what the hindrance was so I looked around to the other side. There stood Gustaf trying to hold on."

Gustaf said, "I was just about to take a tie from the display when someone started to turn it around. I got a bit irritated and held on to it so I could get hold of that tie. Then I saw who it was."

That day ended with a nice dinner at Aquavit.

13 *The dream woman*

It was an unusual dream. No environment, no story – it was all black with the exception of one thing: a television set that seemed to float in the darkness about three metres in front of me, slightly to the left. The screen showed a close-up of a blonde female announcer talking directly to me. I had never seen her before and wondered who she was and what she wanted.

She was charming and seemed rather anxious, as if she wanted to convince me of something. She spoke intently but I could not hear any words or any sound at all. The television was totally silent, but I had a feeling that she wanted to involve me in something, some kind of project. There was also a romantic, slightly erotic undertone.

I watched her, continuing to wonder who she was. Suddenly I became aware of a presence in the darkness just behind me to the left. I sensed a male oriental figure in a bluish kaftan. Strangely enough this did not feel unpleasant or frightening, and there was no feeling of nightmare. On the contrary, the figure felt more like a good and positive, almost loving and protective, presence.

He touched my shoulder and said that this woman would seek contact with me. She would try to get me involved in a certain activity, and also eventually would want to establish a relationship with me. I cannot remember whether I heard his voice or just sensed his thoughts, but what he communicated was very clear. He warned me and said that I should not get involved in any way with the woman. There would be very negative consequences for me if I did. He did not say what would happen, just that it was important.

It did not feel like a threatening command, rather a helpful, friendly warning, like one a parent would offer to a child. His presence was so positive and reassuring that I did not question what he said. I felt a total confidence in him.

He also indicated that she was not an evil woman and had no evil intentions, but that it was important for me to stay away and not get involved.

There the dream ended. It had been unusually lucid and I remembered it clearly when I woke up. But as dreams tend to do, it soon glided into oblivion and was lost.

A couple of months had passed when I got a call from an unknown lady. She told me about a project she was engaged in, a kind of educational set-up that she thought I might be interested in. She sounded knowledgeable and pleasant and knew our company well. What she told me sounded quite interesting, so when she suggested we meet for lunch so she could tell me more, I had no objections. We booked a date for lunch at the Restaurant KB.

I didn't think any more about it until the day arrived and my calendar showed that I had a lunch booked at KB, an excellent restaurant that I and my colleagues often visited. Its interior had remained the same for ages; while many other restaurants in central Stockholm changed their interior every third year or so, trying to establish a new "concept", KB was eternal. When my father visited Stockholm in the 1930s, he liked to go there, and it probably looked exactly the same then as it does today. That kind of atmosphere you cannot create by modern remodelling. I walked towards the restaurant with the usual pleasant anticipation of a good lunch, without particularly thinking about whom I would have for company. I exchanged a few words with the friendly cloakroom attendant and made for the dining room.

In the doorway I stopped in my tracks, almost paralysed. There, by the table with the rounded sofa to the right of the entrance, sat a woman I recognized. I had never seen her in real life, only in the dream. The dream came back and hit me with great clarity. It was the woman in the television! Absolutely no doubt. There she sat. At first I did not know what to do. I could hardly turn around at the door.

Then she saw me. She obviously knew who I was so she waved discreetly to indicate that it was her I was there to meet. I walked up, shook her hand and tried to hide the strange feelings that ravaged my mind.

The conversation proceeded exactly as I knew it would. She told me about the project in a lively and engaged voice. I felt that everything coincided with what the oriental figure in the dream had said. Under normal circumstances I would probably have been interested, but now there was a great big "No!" within me. I did not have to think twice, nor weigh pros and cons; there was no agony of indecision – I knew exactly what my position was. I wish I had that kind of dream a little more often.

Eventually I learnt that the woman is a very competent and engaged person with a good heart, and I have great respect for what she has accomplished over the years.

And I still wonder what would have happened if I had not heeded the warning in the dream.

14 Global Consciousness Project

*Contrary to what everyone knows it may not be
the brain that generates consciousness, but rather
consciousness that makes the brain come forth with
matter, space, time and everything else that we like to
interpret as the physical universe.*

Keith Floyd

Global Consciousness Project (GCP) is the name of
a big research project led by Dr Roger Nelson at Princeton
University. Put simply, it is an attempt to discover whether
or not there exists a collective field of consciousness and,
if so, whether there is a connection between what happens
in that field and what happens in the physical world. The
study started in 1998 and is still in progress, but there are
already results that are considered statistically interesting and
significant.

The study uses small gadgets called Random Event Genera-
tors (REGs). These are a kind of computer circuit that generates an electronic noise through continuous, totally random
sequences of around one thousand ones and zeros per second.

The various REG units are placed all over the world without any connection between them. Instead every REG is individually connected via the internet to a server at Princeton, where the noise is registered in files and stored for analysis. Today there are a great number of such REG units placed in the USA, Europe, Brazil, South Africa, Russia, Japan, China, India, Fiji, New Zealand and Australia.

The electronic noise created by the random dance of the ones and the zeros gives a more or less constant curve, a so-called *bell curve*, which is quite similar in all the units. The curve keeps repeating itself in the same pattern hour after hour, day after day.

But sometimes something strange happens.

When a big international event occurs, something that focuses many people's awareness on one and the same thing, a kind of coherence seems to occur, and the curves of the REGs change dramatically.

A sad but clear example is the attack on the World Trade Center on 11 September 2001. All the 37 REGs that were active that day reacted strongly. The curves changed markedly and the amplitudes were greater than had ever been measured before. These results have been carefully analysed to eliminate any possibility that they could be the result of some statistical abnormality or analytical mistake. The possibility has even eliminated that they could be due to electromagnetic influences from the increased use of mobile phones. (The results were reported in the publication *Foundations of Physics Letters*, vol. 5, no. 6, 2002.)

Over the years the project has been running, thousands of big news events have been analysed and compared to changes in the bell curves. The results are remarkable. They clearly show that thoughts, feelings and intentions actually change the action of the REG units, but there is still no comprehensive theory as to how this is possible.

Intensive work is in progress incorporating theories from many different fields of science, such as *non-linear dynamics, string theory, entropy reduction, information theory, resonance and coherence,* to name just a few.

One of the scientists involved with the project, Dean Radin, who has PhDs in both psychology and electronics, sums it up: "This ongoing experiment suggests that as mass mind moves, so does matter."

Another piece in the synchronicity puzzle?

15 *The outboard motor and the cash register*

I have a friend and fellow jazz musician whose name is Sören Holmström. Sören is a fine drummer who also used to run his own company, DKAB, dealing in shop computers and cash registers. Nowadays he is more into drumsticks than cash registers.

Sören is also the reluctant owner of a motorboat. He likes the practicality and pleasure of his boat when at his summer house in the archipelago. But he dislikes fiddling with the engine, which he feels is always beckoning him to fix something.

One day he was especially fed up with oily fingers, dirty spark plugs and obstinate screws. He decided at last to get some professional help with the engine. Since he did not know of any business in that field, he consulted the yellow pages in the phone book. Among all the companies handling boat engines he chose one named Waxholms Utbordarservice, since it was located in a town by the water not too far from Sören's summer island home.

He picked up the phone and dialled the number. For some reason he remembers that he simultaneously looked at his watch, noticing that it was 11.25 in the morning.

At the other end a recorded voice answered saying that they were closed for lunch between eleven and twelve. Sören put down the receiver without leaving any message. It was too complicated to describe the problem with the erratic behaviour of the engine to a recorder. I'll call back later, he thought, and poured himself a cup of coffee.

Fifteen minutes later the phone rang. It was an unfamiliar man asking about cash registers. Was there possibly a used one for sale? Sören asked about his specific needs and described various models and sizes. They discussed the matter for a while and Sören promised to look into it and call back with more information. He asked for the caller's name and telephone number.

His head began spinning when he heard the answer.

"Waxholm Utbordarservice."

They still take care of Sören's engine when it is wilful, and they still use a cash register from DKAB.

16 *Fredrik's pictures*

Towards the end of the 1980s Fredrik Horn was travelling around the world and had just arrived at the little village of Tanga Loka in Borneo. His travelling companion, Göran Hedelin, who was a photographer, took lots of photographs of the village, which was still pretty much unaffected by tourism and the Western way of life. They were both fascinated to come across a lifestyle that had probably been the same for a thousand years.

Since Fredrik was a writer they discussed compiling a feature about the village and the people. But the more they thought about it the more they decided not to. They did not want to contribute to drawing the attention of the world to something that was still so pristine and untouched by civilization.

Their noble-mindedness was of little consequence. The Western world is the way it is, and only five years later Borneo was a hot tourist destination.

Noticing this, Fredrik decided to write that article after all, and in it make a plea for Tanga Loka to be treated with great care and consideration. He wrote the article and sent it along with lots of photographs to the travel magazine *Vagabond*.

Nothing happened. The story remained unpublished. After some weeks, Fredrik called and asked for his pictures back, well knowing how easily such things get lost at an editorial office. He got the pictures and put them away in some cubbyhole. Years passed and eventually the whole thing was forgotten. Fredrik made new journeys, studied, moved around and tried some different jobs before becoming a copywriter and scriptwriter in Stockholm.

Many years later, in November 2000, Fredrik's father called and said that he would be coming to Stockholm the following week. He had moved to the south of Sweden, and told Fredrik that he had found a box full of photographs that he thought belonged to Fredrik and that he would bring it with him to Stockholm.

Fredrik had no idea what those pictures were, but said, "Fine, bring the box and I'll take a look at them." When he got the box he found that it contained all the pictures from the Borneo trip of many years earlier. He had not seen them or thought about them for years, and had no idea where they had been. How nice that they should pop up again after all these years, he thought, and put the box on a table so he would not forget to take them to his old travelling friend, whom he was to meet a couple of days later. They would have a nice time reliving old memories of Borneo.

Three days later the telephone rang. It was the editor-in-chief of *Vagabond* magazine.

"You wrote an article on Borneo for us many years ago. We would like to publish it now, but we have no pictures. Do you possibly still have the pictures you took on that trip, or do you happen to know where they could be found?"

He did know. A few days earlier he would not have known. But now, just before the magazine called and asked about them, they had popped up from nowhere and after many years in hiding were sitting on his table.

A few months later I received the following story from Fredrik, who had now begun paying attention to these kinds of events. He gave it to me in writing, so with Fredrik's permission I will just reproduce it here. He was working as a copywriter at an advertising agency at the time.

A girl had called Janet at the reception desk and asked whether she could come and show her portfolio to a copywriter. Karin (another copywriter at the same agency) and I discussed who would attend the meeting, and it fell on me.

The girl's name is Linda and she arrived this morning. We began small-talking about this and that, and I immediately felt that we got along fine and that she was a person with whom it was very easy to communicate. An hour later we were still sitting there talking about everything between heaven and earth.

I asked about her education, and it was a bit funny to find that we had both graduated from the same high school. I was not surprised since it is a big school, and I have met many people over the years who had studied there. But then I asked where she came from and she answered Viggbyholm. This was getting interesting. Having leaned back earlier, I now bent forward and said: "I am from Viggbyholm too."

Simultaneously we both said, "Värtavägen." "Yes, that is the street where I grew up, Värtavägen number six," said Linda. My jaws fell open. "That´s where I grew up too," I said. "My parents actually built that house. My room was just above the garage."

"That was mine too!" she almost screamed.

We just sat there looking at each other, finding the whole thing hard to believe. It felt as if we were siblings. Linda is twelve years younger than me. I had moved out when her parents bought the house from my parents thirteen years ago. Linda and I had thus grown up on exactly the same square metres for at least ten years, we are both copywriters and she came to show me her portfolio.

My old room has thus brought forth two copywriters. It must be the most copywriter-dense place in Sweden. I wonder what the next person in that room will do.

17 Just an idea

There are only two ways to live your life.
As if nothing is a miracle, or as if everything
is a miracle.

Albert Einstein

The Soviet empire crashed under the weight of its own absurdity. The system of thought, the way of seeing the world that called itself Communism, suddenly lay there in its own smoking ruins. One of its most obvious and grotesque creations was the Berlin Wall.

A few days after the fall of the Wall there was a big sign on a house on the eastern side of the border, close to the passage known as Checkpoint Charlie. There was a big portrait of Karl Marx and beneath it someone had written: "Sorry, chaps, it was just an idea."

This whole historical spectacle that had cost so many millions of human lives, and held whole nations under inhuman oppression, was actually nothing more than an idea. Just an idea.

Ideas rule the world. Ideas about good and bad, right and

wrong, allowed and forbidden. Ideas about what life is, about how people should behave and about how the universe is constructed. Ideas about which religion is the only truth, about what political dogma is the only one that works, and about how the economic system should be organized. Everything is basically just ideas.

People have always had thoughts and beliefs about reality. Perhaps we must in order to exist. But at the same time they control us from morning to night. They have an uncanny power over our minds. Sometimes they are stronger than life itself.

Al-Qaeda terrorists sacrificed their own and thousands of others people's lives when they flew into World Trade Center. Why? Just an idea?

A Kurdish father shot to death his own daughter because she wanted to marry a Swedish boy. She "dishonoured" the family. The girl's life was taken because a certain idea occupied the father's mind. There was no objective fact, no scientific studies showing that the family was dishonoured. It was just an idea.

People of Northern Ireland calling themselves Protestants fought against other similar humans calling themselves Catholics. For many years they hated, shot, blasted and hurt each other. Why? Just ideas.

Some ideas may feel quite natural and self-evident. I could not, for instance, bring myself to kill another human being. The idea from the Ten Commandments, "Thou shalt not kill", is deeply ingrained in most of us. But a philosopher could easily challenge me and question whether I really stand by that. Philosophers often have the ability to take apart our most cherished ideas. I could, for example, be asked what I would do if a killer held a gun to the head of my child, and I had a weapon trained on him. The only chance to save my child's life would be to shoot him first. I would not hesitate for a second. The idea that my child's life is more important than a killer's life would without doubt win over the idea that thou shall not kill. Thus we can harbour quite contrary ideas in our minds, and which one dominates for the moment depends on what situation we are in.

A thinking person can accept that it is so. But not a fundamentalist. He is totally consumed by one single idea and blind to the possibility that there could be another way of thinking. It is a comfortable position, quite attractive to some. You are liberated from the effort of thinking for yourself. You achieve a distinct identity instead of the rickety self-image you might have had before. You get a feeling of belonging to something important, a feeling that you might have lacked before. You shut off all questioning and let yourself go for "the cause". That is what makes fundamentalism so dangerous, wherever it appears, whatever form it takes.

We harbour many beliefs without even being aware of them, while others can be a very conscious choice. One idea, for example, says that when we die it is all over and there is no continuation of consciousness, no afterlife of any kind, just a black nothingness. Another idea says the exact opposite, that when we die our consciousness just leaves the physical body as if getting out of a taxi, and the core of our existence continues in another dimension.

I can see that both ideas are possible and that there are no hard facts proving either one of the two positions. But in recent years there has been a marked increase in what is called "survival research", and more and more circumstantial evidence seems to support the belief that life in some form continues after our physical death. So that is the position I choose.

No matter how much I think about death, I cannot reach

any conclusion other than that it must be a transformation from one state to another. Just an idea, sure, but it is an idea decidedly more pleasant to live with than the alternative.

I have made the same choice about synchronicities. You can decide that any event, any coincidence, regardless of how strange it may seem, can be explained through statistics, mathematics and the law of cause and effect. Nothing miraculous at all. Or you can regard synchronicities as the result of some sort of interplay between the material and the non-material worlds, between spirit and matter, the Field and our individual lives. Quite miraculous.

That too is just an idea. But it is also the one I choose.

18 *The accelerator*

I was on the road in my Pontiac Transport to a small town in the south of Sweden. My friend, the piano player and Psycho-Synthesis teacher Stig Löfstrand, and I were to play a small jazz concert at a conference where he was a speaker. The Pontiac was perfect for transporting a double bass, amplifier and various other stuff. I was in a hurry. As usual I had not started early enough and was anxious about not being late for the concert.

I was racing as fast as I dared on the motorway when it happened. The accelerator suddenly went totally limp. The engine dropped to idling and the speed to about five kilometres per hour. I stepped on the gas but the pedal just hung loose and hit the floor without any reaction from the engine. I had never experienced anything like it and wondered what had gone wrong. In the field of car mechanics I am close to being mentally handicapped. What the heck should I do? I couldn't crawl like this on a busy highway. I steered as close as possible to the edge of the road to get out of the way of the traffic and slowly crept forward, getting strange looks from the drivers swishing by. Damn! I didn't have time for this! Why did it have to happen just now? I'd miss the concert. Shit!

Then suddenly that other feeling, that other awareness,

appeared. Alongside the stressed and upset part of me there was a thought: "Be calm, don't worry. It will sort itself out. It will be fine." I could not understand, in the middle of my misery, how this problem would be solved, yet I felt a kind of trust in the universe, almost a curiosity. What would happen next?

At the same moment my eyes caught sight of a small turn-off to the right, and I realized that I had to take it in order to get off the highway and contemplate my situation. The car crept slowly along the roadside to the turn-off, which involved a sharp right turn. It curved down on to a smaller road that led into a tunnel under the highway. I must stop somewhere on the other side of that tunnel, I thought. There must be a solution.

As I slowly came out on the other side, there was a revelation. A Statoil petrol station! What luck! So that was the answer. Slowly, slowly, I rolled into the station, happy and relieved that the solution was so close.

So close but yet so far away. I found out that the only staff at the station was a cashier, and all she knew was how to charge for gas, definitely not how to fix a broken accelerator.

"No, there is no mechanic here today."

Strange. I had felt that the problem was about to be solved, but that was obviously wrong. Big disappointment. I thought about Stig and the concert audience and the shame of not being there on time. Panic started to take hold again. What to do now?

At that moment a rugged voice came from a man standing just behind me in the line to the cashier. "You need a mechanic?"

I turned around and saw a rather chubby man in a taxi driver's uniform.

"Yes," I said. "The accelerator gave up on me and I have no idea how to fix it."

"No problem. My pal has a repair shop just five minutes from here. I'll call him on my mobile phone. I'm a cab driver and my car is just outside."

He went to his car and took out his mobile phone. Only a few minutes later a breakdown van rolled into the petrol station. It was his friend, who happened to be in the neighbourhood. He took a look at my accelerator, fetched a few tools and three minutes later the pedal was fixed. He didn't say anything, but I could see what he thought about my mechanical talents.

I was immensely grateful to both the taxi driver and the mechanic, and to the universe which had once more come to my rescue. I asked the mechanic how much I owed him. He hesitated – he wasn't sure since it was such an easy thing to fix. To him, yes, but to me it was a miracle, so I gave him a couple of hundred kronor, which at first he vaguely protested about. But I insisted. I thanked the cab driver too and felt a great relief when I was back on the highway heading at full speed towards the concert.

Ten to twelve minutes had passed since my car had become useless.

I arrived in time for the concert.

19 *The confirmation*

It was 11.30, nearly lunchtime. The thought struck me that it would be nice to have lunch with Catherine, my wife, who was at home with our two-year-old son Oliver. It rarely happened that we had lunch together on a regular working day, but today I had no lunch appointments, so why not?

I called home. Nobody there. I left a message on the answering machine and said that we could do it some other day instead.

Fifteen minutes later Catherine called from her mobile phone.

"Hello, where are you?" I asked.

"Oliver and I are in the car headed for downtown."

"So where are you going, what's up?"

"We are on our way to have lunch with you."

"Oh, fine, so you got my message, then."

"No, what message?"

She had not received the message but had had the same idea as I, and had decided to go into town.

We met at Plates, the salad bar located in the NK department store.

During our conversation we touched on the big question of what was really important in life. What did I desire beyond obvious things like health and the welfare of the family? What material things were most important to me, and what could I live without? We talked about cars and boats and the like, but nothing felt really necessary. If I could choose only two things, what would they be? I thought hard about what was most important to me.

Two parts of my life emerged as more important than others. One was my study with my books. I like the nearness of books, and I don't think it is just because both my father and my grandfather were booksellers. I love the feeling that there on the bookshelves is stored an immense body of human knowledge, wisdom and creativity, gathered and accessible to me at any time. That was something I did not want be without. My library would definitely be one of my choices.

Another need that has grown gradually stronger over the years is to potter about in the garden. The nearness of the soil, all its expressions of life, being a partner with nature, appeal to me more and more. There is a special kind of truth in nature that does not exist in a city office. A big stone, a tree, a handful of earth are immeasurably much more real than most of the stuff you're dealing with in an office, especially in the media world. It had become a way for me to literally get grounded. The garden was my escape, not *from* but *to* reality.

It wasn't always like that. I grew up with the belief that sailing was the meaning of life. My dad often cited the Latin motto *"Navigare necesse est"* and did his best to live by it. He also used to say that there are only two honest professions in the world, those of farmer and seaman. There was no doubt on which side he counted himself. He felt much more satisfied and at home in the cockpit of his sailing boat than behind the counter of his bookshop.

That early conditioning had made me, as a grown-up

married man, move to Österskär, a very boat-minded community north of Stockholm. Everybody who lived in Österskär was a boat person. You lived there simply because of the closeness to the sea – you were already halfway into the archipelago. The size of my own boats had over the years, increased from one not much bigger than a dinghy to a fair-sized sailing yacht. It went without saying in Österskär that as soon as your finances allowed, you changed to a bigger boat.

In those days, when we moved to our new house, I could see the difference between a tree and a lawn, but my horticultural proficiency didn't stretch much farther than that. Gradually, though, I began feeling a certain attraction to the green stuff out there. Eventually I even planted a few bushes and established a small vegetable plot.

The garden and the boat began more and more to compete for my time and attention. Especially in the spring, when there were a lot of things to do in the garden, and there was also a lot of work involved in preparing the boat. The farmer in me had started to grow and was now beginning to play king of the hill with the sailor.

Suddenly one day the struggle was over. It was the middle of July.

In heavy rain and wind we had anchored at a pristine island for the night. Around three o'clock in the morning I woke up, conscious of the boat thumping against rock. The anchor had been dragging under the wind pressure. Crawling outside in miserable weather and darkness at three o'clock to fix the moorings is no fun. It has no resemblance to the dreams you have in February and March about gorgeous sailing trips in wonderful vacation weather.

It was still raining and windy when we sailed away in the morning, and the temperature was a miserable 9 degrees

Celsius, which sank even lower in the wind and wetness. I sat alone at the rudder, shivering in my rainwear. The whole atmosphere in the boat was at a low point. My wife and kids sat in the cabin sulking. Patrik and Peter because they hadn't found any friends to play with on that little island, and my wife because I hadn't reduced the sails enough and the boat was listing too much.

The rain whipped my face. Navigation was difficult because the chart was flapping in the wind and the rainy haze erased all the contours of the surrounding islands. I had a tough job fending off the erratic gusts of wind that sometimes pressed the boat down so that the gunwale was at water level. I would rather have been poking about in the garden.

I suddenly became aware of an intense inner dialogue. It was as if it took place quite independently of my own morose thoughts, and I was reduced to a listener to a short conversation between two inner voices.

One said: "Is this happiness?"

The other answered immediately and emphatically: "NO!"

At that moment my identity shifted from sailor to farmer. I turned the boat around, changed course and headed for home. This resulted in a more open wind, so the boat straightened up and the sailing became much more calm. The family looked out and wondered what had happened. Everybody thought it was a wise decision.

Having arrived home, I drafted an ad about a sailing boat for sale and after a week it was sold. In Österskär it goes without saying that if you sell a boat it is because you are buying a bigger one. Neighbours and friends were interested and asked, "What will it be now?"

"I'm not going to have a boat any more."

"Oh, come on, what will it be? An Omega 42? A Scanmar 35?"

"I'm not buying anything. I'm through with sailing."

"Aah, don't be silly. Tell me, what are you looking for?"

The thought of not having a boat was not tenable in Öster-skär. It was totally unthinkable, impossible. A boat in the harbour was as natural as a television in the living room. Some may have thought that I had run into financial troubles, some that I had lost my marbles. Occasionally I wondered myself whether I had really done the right thing, but all doubts disappeared one Sunday morning the following spring.

I was relaxed and enjoying myself, poking about in what was to become a new vegetable plot. My nearest neighbour, the bank manager, was busy painting the bottom of his boat down by the wharf. But since it was a pretty cold day, the paint thickened, so he had to come home once every half-hour to warm it up. While the paint was warming up he climbed up and down a ladder to the roof to change some broken tiles. I saw him come rushing with the paint into the house, then out of the house, up the ladder, down the ladder, into the house, out again, driving off in the car, and so it went on all morning. Once, when he came hurrying back, stressed and red in the face, he caught sight of me standing there calmly on the other side of the fence. He rushed on, red eyed, hair on end, and without stopping he shouted: "You're so fucking industrious!"

Then I knew that I had made the right decision. Being a farmer suited me just fine – a feeling that would only grow stronger with time. So twenty years later, during that lunch at Plates, there was no doubt that a garden was the second thing I did not want to live without. I felt that the two choices, a library and a garden, were precisely what I desired most of all of material things. A lot of other stuff I could do without.

As I got home that evening, I picked up the day's mail from the kitchen table. Among the letters was a piece of direct mail from a book club. I held it in my hand, contemplating dropping it directly into the wastepaper basket, but an impulse made me open it. I pulled out the contents and immediately my eyes were drawn to a couple of lines at the bottom of a page. It was as if they left the page and floated up towards my eyes. It was a quote from Cicero: "He who owns a library and a garden lacks nothing."

I couldn't help but wave towards the ceiling and thank whoever it was that had given me such a nice confirmation.

20 Cause and effect

The world appears to us not as a blind play of atoms, but instead as a big organisation.

Marilyn Ferguson

It seems obvious that everything has a cause. If you have a dent in your car there is a clear cause. You were either hit by another car or you hit something yourself. We live safe in the assumption that reality is like a big machine in which one cog influences another cog that influences a shaft that influences a wheel, and so on. Whatever happens, we can find the reason behind it. It is called *causality*, the law of cause and effect.

Thus you could say that a synchronistic event can be explained by the causes behind it. The fact that that particular Cicero quote should be in that particular letter that reached me on that particular day had its simple causes. The timing of the book club campaign was just planned that way, our address was on their mailing list, and the person who created the mailing had happened to find that quote and thought it was appropriate for the campaign. Clear *causal* facts. Nothing strange at all. The fact that we had been talking about exactly the same thing on the same day was a "pure coincidence".

But to me it was more than that. The narrow, causal view of synchronicity is trapped in time, space and matter. I suspect that synchronistic events might be born in quite a different manner. The law of cause and effect works fine when it is about something so limited as a machine or a mechanical system. But life is hardly just a mechanical system.

I don't think you can explain synchronicity just by the law of cause and effect. I am not even sure it is good enough to explain any event at all.

Every event has not one but many causes, which in turn have a lot of other causes, and the whole thing gets lost in a boundless net of causes and effects. The causal connections grow into an impossible tangle, which it is pointless to try to sort out.

My brother Torbjörn was a pilot living in the south of Sweden. My daughter Jana, who was thirteen at the time, had been visiting Uncle Torbjörn and his wife Deisa during a school holiday. On the trip back to Stockholm she was invited to sit with him in the cockpit. She was a little nervous and said: "We are not going to crash now, Uncle Torbjörn, are we?"

"My dear Jana," said Torbjörn, calming her, "I have been flying for thirty years and have never crashed. The risk of us crashing is much less than the risk that you will have a collision on the way home from the airport."

That is exactly what happened. They didn't crash and we had a collision on the way home. I picked up Jana at the airport and suddenly the roads were iced over and treacherously slippery. We were on a straight stretch of road when the car in front of us, a Suzuki, suddenly started to sway and spin out of control. It went round and round, over to the opposite side of the road, kept spinning, swayed back on to our side again, and eventually came to rest facing backwards with the left rear wheel a bit off the road and the front facing us.

I tried to brake carefully and not lose control myself. It was impossible to stop immediately with my summer tyres, and I could not pass the unfortunate car since there was a lot of oncoming traffic. The driver of the Suzuki must have had a guardian angel not to have collided with an oncoming car when spinning around out there on the opposite side. The traffic on this road was usually pretty dense.

I couldn't quite stop my car but had to turn on to the verge as far as possible to avoid a frontal collision. When it was all over the left corner of my front bumper had made a small dent in the left front door of the Suzuki.

I got out and found a young woman behind the wheel. She sat motionless with her hands over her face. It was impossible to communicate with her. The door was jammed and wouldn't open. I went over and opened the right-hand door to see whether she was injured, but found that she was just shocked. Eventually she calmed down and we could begin the tedious exchange of insurance details.

How could this event be explained by cause and effect? One of the causes was the slippery ice that had formed on the road. The cause of the ice was a sudden drop in temperature. The cause of the drop in temperature was a cold front that just had passed. The cause of the cold front was a low pressure system that had formed north of the Faroe islands. The cause of the low pressure system was a change in the jetstream over the Atlantic. The cause of the jetstream change was a fluctuation in the Humboldt current off California. The cause of that was … and so on for all eternity.

But this complicated background to the slippery road was

just a small part of the net of causes behind our collision. There were a lot of other causes too. Each one was itself just a small part of its own net of causal connections.

For instance, the fact that we were in that exact spot when the Suzuki started to spin. One of the reasons for that was that Torbjörn had landed at a certain time. That in turn was caused by another network of cause and effect: the baggage handling at the point of departure, the number of passengers to be handled, refuelling, the slot time for the flight, the wind conditions, the ground service, air traffic control and lots of other factors. Each such influence was in turn influenced by its own infinite network of causes and effects.

Then it took a certain time for Torbjörn and Jana to get to the terminal. I went to the bathroom, thereby delaying our trip home by a couple of minutes. The cause of that effect was probably that I had had a big cup of coffee before I left home. The traffic lights were timed the way they were for unknown reasons. The traffic at that particular time had a certain density; our speed was influenced by hundreds of other cars that happened to be on our route for a thousand different reasons. Just driving through the city means that you are influenced by a virtually incalculable network of causal connections.

A further cause of the collision was that the woman in her Suzuki was driving at exactly that spot at exactly that time. What complicated network of causes and effects was behind that fact? You can go on like that for ever; it never ends.

I guess our little collision was not a particularly synchronistic event. It is at any rate difficult to find anything specifically meaningful in it – that is, if I don't choose to interpret it as a message to drive more carefully. Anyway, if this little event is virtually impossible to analyse with the help of simple cause-and-effect reasoning, how impossible is it then to understand a truly synchronistic and meaningful event? At least, as long as you stay confined within the walls of the mechanistic world view.

Every event is like the midpoint in a gigantic spider web whose threads fork out and spread in all directions. Each thread has contributed to that particular event, but is at the same time the result of an infinite number of other events. The net becomes like a field where everything influences everything else. How, then, is it possible in this mess to find a simple causal connection? No matter how hard you try you can grasp only a fraction of the total reality. Most of it remains unknown.

Who can tell what is and what is not in this great, unknown field? Perhaps there are powers that influence events, not in a mechanistic, machine-like way, but in a way that has more to do with energy, information, feelings and intentions.

There is said to be an old ritual among the Aborigines, the indigenous people of Australia, whereby someone can get help from a shaman to get rid of an undesirable person. People gather around the shaman, who holds a piece of bone, probably human, dances around, chants, goes into a trance and utters magical invocations. Suddenly he stops and points the piece of bone towards the undesirable one.

This man immediately starts to get sick. He has difficulty breathing, gets convulsions, his body dehydrates and after three days he is usually dead. I have heard that the government of Australia has even passed a law that forbids Aborigines pointing at somebody with a piece of bone. It is classified as raising a deadly weapon.

What is cause and effect in a case like that? You can hardly find it on a mechanistic, material level. The shaman never even touches the undesirable one. What happens occurs on a quite different level.

21 *The road to Bäckastrand*

After many years of living in Lidingö we considered this island suburb of Stockholm our home town. We had tried different kinds of accommodation – apartment, villa, looked at lots of houses for sale – but had never quite found our ultimate home, not quite reached that feeling of "this is it", this is where we want to stay and belong. We now lived in a rather nice house by the Kottla lake. There were no tangible reasons to complain, but still the feeling lingered that this was something temporary, this was not where our roots would grow deep into the soil.

Occasionally we touched on the dream of finding a good plot and building our own house, but we never got around to initiating the search, much less driving around looking at plots for sale. Yet the idea was there somewhere as a vague feeling that one day something would happen.

My interest in gardening could not bloom in the present house. The plot was quite small with a shady little lawn facing the north-east. It did not give me much inspiration; there was simply nothing to do. This was quite intentional and one of the reasons we had moved here. At that time we had a summer house with a big plot in the archipelago, and two demanding gardens would have been too much, even for my somewhat erratic but at times intensive gardening activities.

Therefore this house with its small lawn was ideal.

But now the situation had changed. We had sold the summer house, so all I had was that dark little piece of lawn, and my garden activities were at a low ebb. Until one day in April.

The weather was nice, and an irresistible longing for the soil came over me suddenly and unexpectedly. I felt a strong desire to do something and, without any plan as to what exactly I was going to do, I pulled on my boots and went out to grab hold of something, anything. There is always something you can do in a garden, no matter how small it is, I told myself.

Well, once I was standing on the shady little lawn I found myself just staring at the neighbour's wall. What could I do here? I stood for a long while, totally inactive, without finding one meaningful little thing to do.

Suddenly I was hit by another, much stronger feeling. It was totally unexpected, almost like a ray of light or energy that entered my head and shook my consciousness. I was totally consumed by the thought: "Now, damn it! Now is the time! Now we have to start looking around for somewhere new!"

I ran into the house, excited, pulled off my boots and shouted for Catherine, who was on the upper floor. "Catherine, we must start looking now! If we don't do anything, nothing will happen! Come, let's look in the newspaper!" I tore open the *Svenska Dagbladet* and hastily flipped through the pages to find the property ads. I called again: "Catherine, come on!" The unusual anxiety in my voice made her wonder what had happened to me. She hurried down the stairs to see what was wrong, and looked at me quizzically.

"We must start looking," I said. "Plots for sale. See what's out there."

Catherine looked a bit surprised at my sudden enthusiasm.

She came up and looked rather half-heartedly over my shoulder. "Look," she said, and pointed at a very small advertisement of just two lines that I hadn't even noticed: SEASIDE, LIDINGÖ, and a telephone number.

Well, well, I thought. Sure, we aimed high, but my dreams did not fly quite as high as to aspire to a true seaside place. "It is probably some dark steep cliff facing north that they are trying to glamorize, calling it seaside," I said.

We looked for more ads without finding anything interesting, but my eyes kept coming back to that first little ad. Somehow it had achieved a certain lustre on the page. Finally we decided to check it out anyway. Why not do it as a little Saturday trip with the kids, and at the same time try out the new car, a white Volvo 850 that had been delivered just a few days earlier.

When we drove away, seven-year-old Oliver said: "Could you not say that this is our maiden trip with the new car?"

"Yes, that's exactly what it is," I said, charmed by and proud of his bright mind.

"I hope the same thing won't happen to us that happened to *Wasa*," said Oliver.

Wasa was the proud Swedish battleship, the mightiest warship of the Baltic Sea. Newly built, she had left the wharf for her maiden voyage in the year 1628 to impress the world with her power. After only a few minutes she heeled over, water rushing in through all the open gun ports, and sank dramatically in the middle of Stockholm harbour. She was salvaged in 1961 and is now the main attraction at the Wasa Museum in Stockholm.

I was amused by Oliver's association and decided to drive extra carefully. I had no idea that this little trip would change our lives in a quite different manner.

Eventually we found our way through a wooded area along

a small dirt road to the house of the seller. It had a beautiful location by a sea inlet. Not facing north at all, as I had suspected, but south-west, the ideal point of the compass for a seaside house. The plot for sale was a large area partitioned off from his estate. The seller was a friendly, middle-aged man who had lived here since childhood, when his father and uncle had managed the two boatyards located in the bay.

There was no agent involved. The new plot was a so-called pure seaside property, which, according to the old map, stretched all the way out to the middle of the bay. A small red cottage and a couple of sheds strengthened the impression of absolute idyll.

It felt almost sacred to walk around there enjoying the stillness, the view, the nature. I felt a strange excitement that was further strengthened by the kids' enjoyment. "I want to live here, Daddy!" "Buy this place!" My excitement was somewhat tempered by the high price and the other prospective buyers who were also walking around there. I also had a vague feeling that it was too good to be true, that I was probably not worthy of something this great.

I wonder how often we miss out on life's opportunities because of feelings like that. They are often not quite conscious, but have a great influence on the choices we make in life; "I am not worth it" sneaks around in our subconscious and keeps us from getting what is within our reach. Usually that kind of hidden belief emanates from childhood conditioning. Perhaps I had been naughty and was told "You are not worth it" when I wanted that piece of candy.

I knew about these things from my studies with the Gestalt Academy, but they are tricky and have a way of sneaking past your defences. Now, fortunately, I managed to catch them and keep them at bay.

We thanked the seller and went back home, but the whole family had been affected by the excitement. We could not let go of the image of the glittering sea and the beautiful nature round about. We discussed pros and cons, counted and calculated and occasionally allowed ourselves to say "what if ..." and "how would it be if ..." The kids had no doubts. That was where they wanted to live.

After a few days of kicking pros and cons back and forth, we called the seller and asked to come for a second look. I feared that the place would surely be sold already, but evidently not. We were welcome to take another look.

This time we were alone walking around, seeing more and more lovely details. The shoreline featured soft rocks, a small beach and a pier. Behind the site was a forested area. No traffic passed by since the little dirt road ended at the edge of the site. It was situated right between the forest and the sea. The trees, the bushes, the sheds – everything breathed idyll. The whole place felt unusually harmonious, with a noticeable element of silence, one of the most overlooked luxuries in our time, as well as being in very short supply. We gradually fell in love with the place.

A few more weeks of intensive pondering, calculations and discussions with the seller followed. Strangely enough the competition did not seem too fierce. We soon understood why. The area was not yet city-planned. The city was about to begin a planning process in the coming autumn, and no one knew where that would lead. It was entirely possible that we would never get a building permit for this wonderful site. Besides, there was no communal water and sewerage system. There were rumours that the city had some plans to install one, but it was impossible to get any confirmation. I had my fill of things to worry about. What if we bought it and then could not build a new house? The primitive little cottage of about fifty square metres was hardly usable as a family house. It might instead turn out to be an extremely expensive summer house.

"Don't worry, it will work itself out," said Catherine. "I can feel it."

She is not a foolhardy person – rather, wise and judicious – so I was surprised at her confidence. But I was also influenced by it, so I continued the discussions with the seller about various details, not least the price. Sometimes I would get attacked by anguish, but Catherine's calm optimism helped keep me on track. On 4 June we signed the contract.

I turned the cottage into a writer's den and little by little we began thinking about plans to build a house. But we had to wait for the city plan. And hope. When the local government people came around, surveying the area, I invited them for coffee and gave an inspired speech about our dreams for the new house, and our plans to make it totally ecological. I believe I did a good job, perhaps aided by what Henry Kissinger once said about a political proposition: "It has the added advantage of being true."

The area is very special in that it feels and looks totally rural, like some place far out in the archipelago. Yet it is only fifteen to twenty minutes by car from the very centre of Stockholm city. All houses in the area have names, in the old-fashioned way, there are no street numbers. A small brook flows across our site from the forest to the rear, and into the sea by the beach, so we baptized the place Bäckastrand, which had also been the name of my mother's childhood home. (In Swedish it denotes brook and beach.)

About a year later the local government presented its new area plan, which would determine whether or not we would be allowed to build a house. We had made a big gamble. What would we do if we lost? I didn't even want to think about it.

There were seven old houses in the area. The partitioning of our plot was perhaps the only change that had occurred in almost a century, and the new plan detailed every one of the plots, which now had become eight. About ours it said: "Can suitably be used for building a house for permanent living."

Bingo! And soon thereafter construction of the communal water and sewerage infrastructure to serve the houses along our little dirt road began. Catherine's optimism had been well founded – everything had fallen into place and we were now free to begin creating our own private paradise.

The journey had actually begun in a much stranger way than we knew, from the beginning. The seller told us that for many years he had wanted to partition this part of his large site, but the authorities had always said no. He had stubbornly kept renewing his application year after year, and suddenly one day, out of the blue, he was given his permit. He hurried to get the land surveyor to execute the partition, and as soon as it was done he put a small ad in the paper. It was the very ad we had seen in the only newspaper we happened to have at home that day in April, when I had the irresistible urge to start looking.

It was published only on that day, only in that newspaper.

22 *Three problems – one solution*

Problem no. 1

An acute attack of overbearing presumptuousness had made me buy a Steinway grand piano, a so-called C model, a monster built for big concert halls. It really was not my intention, but when I was going off on the hunt for a grand piano I asked my friend and piano player Stig Löfstrand to come along and help me choose. It is always wise to seek expert advice when you are going to buy something expensive. What I had in mind was a more common, so-called A-model, but there was none that met with Stig's approval. Grand pianos are not exactly your staple commodity in the store. Stig tried out what they had and found a B-model that he thought was quite OK. A B-model is a good deal bigger than an A-model, but not as big as a C-model. He laid out some chords over the keyboard and listened with a tilted head. Sure, it was fine, a very good instrument.

I looked at the big and beautiful grand and tried to visualize it in our living room. I fantasized about the old-fashioned musical soirées I had planned to arrange at home. Not to mention the joy of the piano players when we had jam sessions. I tinkled a little myself and thought it sounded great.

Then Stig sat down at the big monster, the C-model – there

was only one – and started to play. I saw him disappear into another world altogether with "Round Midnight" and "Ruby, My Dear". I think that Thelonius Monk's tunes, for those who can play them, are especially useful when it comes to revealing the qualities of a piano, or lack thereof.

"Oooh, aah," was heard from Stig, and sure, the piano sounded wonderful. What else would you expect from a concert grand piano? But you can't buy a beast like that for a normal home. Now he must stop playing and start talking, I thought.

Stig was lyrical. "That one there," he said and pointed at the B-model, "that is a very good instrument. But this one," he played a few chords on the monster, "this is more than an instrument, this is something you fall in love with. That one," he pointed at the B-model, "is a good grand piano, but this," he laid out a beautiful chord on the C-model, "this is love."

I lack rationality and logic when it comes to music, so a few days later the big, magnificent instrument was delivered to my home. Fortunately the living room was rather large so it fitted in without problems. Even my own fumbling on the keyboard sounded good.

That it was an exquisite instrument was confirmed one evening when we had the only musical soirée that ever came to pass. My friend and teacher, the bass player Red Mitchell, had given a series of concerts in Sweden together with the American piano player Roger Kellaway, and they had an evening to spare. I took the chance and engaged them. We invited all our friends and acquaintances who liked music to a real musical soirée.

Red and Roger enthralled us with great live music, and Roger was obviously enamoured of the grand piano. On one tune he played a concluding cadence that rolled down towards the lowest notes. Suddenly he stopped playing, stood up abruptly, looked into the strings under the open lid, bowed deeply and said: "Thank you."

A few years later we had moved to the house by the lake, where the living room was not as large. The grand piano occupied almost a third of the room. Granted, it was played on now and then, but more and more I began seeing it with new eyes. How could I justify having a professional instrument that was not used professionally? How could I let it so totally dominate our quite ordinary living room? Was it not a bit silly having a giant Steinway concert piano in a regular-sized house? The room would be much more harmonious with a small A-model. The thought matured gradually: I ought to switch, I ought to sell it and buy an A-model instead.

But how would I do that? I aired my problem with the piano company, who pretended to be concerned and understanding, but they were definitely not interested in buying it back. They would be delighted to sell me an A-model, but to take on the C piano, no, that was too difficult. It was hard to find a buyer for such an instrument. You bet. How many private individuals have money enough, and craziness enough, to follow my example? Maybe in a year or so there would be an institution somewhere in Europe that might be interested in a concert grand piano. But how would I find it, if it existed at all? I did not know where to begin, so I just let it go. Some day it would sort itself out.

Problem no. 2

We had bought the new plot but not started building yet. I used the little red cottage as a writer's den. My gardening interest got an extra boost from the exciting possibilities I imagined laid out there waiting on the pristine ground. I often left my desk to go out and stroll among the wild trees and bushes. Here you could have a vegetable patch, there a dam, a hedge along here. It felt big, much bigger than my horticultural knowledge. I would need help, at least some good advice. I did not want a landscape architect to come and plan everything. I wanted to have my own say in the matter. But I wanted to find some knowledgeable person whom I could consult, in order not to start something that would be doomed from the beginning.

But who? I was not familiar enough with the gardening world and did not know any such person. Where do you find someone like that?

One evening I was zapping between the channels on the television. Suddenly there was a man standing by an apple tree with pruning shears in his hand. I stopped immediately to see what this was all about. He spoke very nicely about plants and gardens and I immediately felt that this was exactly the kind of guy I would like to meet and consult about my garden-to-be. He was just right, but who was he? Eventually it transpired that his name was Lars Krantz. I managed to jot down the name but missed the details of where he worked or where he came from. Wherever he was I wanted to get in touch with him. I searched the phone book and found a couple of guys with the same name, but none of them was the right one. I simply couldn't find that nice gardener from the television screen.

Well, heck, I stopped looking. The problem was not acute. Sooner or later I'd find him.

Problem no. 3

It had been a great relief to get the statement from the authorities that our site could "suitably be used for building a house for permanent living". The previous insecurity had surely had the advantage of scaring away some competing buyers when the plot was for sale. But now it was all in place. Time to start talking with an architect, but which one? I consulted my old friend and business partner Lars Hall. If there is anyone who knows about architects and has clear opinions, he is the one. I know of no one who is more aesthetically aware than Lars. His advice would be valuable.

Yes, he had a strong recommendation, an architect he had worked with himself and was very pleased with. This architect was skilful, experienced and kept things in good order. It sounded perfect, and Lars arranged a meeting. We met with a very pleasant architect who obviously had a good track record and knew what he was doing. Added to that Lars's own good experiences of working with him, and we had no objections. Of course he was the man.

That is what the intellect said. The rational mind found no reason for doubt. Everything looked right. But deep down the intuition stirred a bit. There was another signal, vague and unclear, but strong enough to make me feel a little bit worried. Is this really right? But the rational mind was there immediately and suppressed the feeling. Of course I feel a certain angst, it is such an important decision, this project means so much to me, but that feeling is nothing to worry about. How lucky we were that Lars knew this architect.

The usual old battle took place between the intellect and the intuition. Once again the intellect won. And once again it was wrong.

The architect came and looked at the site. We told him about our intentions and hopes, and he began sketching ideas. We had more meetings and discussions, looked at more sketches, pondering all the hundreds of questions that pop up which you never thought of before, but which you have to resolve quickly when you are about to build a house. More meetings, more pondering, and a nagging feeling that we were on the wrong track without exactly knowing what the right track was. Catherine shared the feeling. We could not pinpoint what it was, but the feeling grew stronger.

Maybe it was an impossible task to design a house that would meet all our wishes. It should harmonize with nature and the environment. It should be discreet and not call out "look at me" across the bay. It should be ecological. It should be a synthesis between Swedish archipelago and Japanese monastery.

The days passed and the architect's fee was mounting.

The solution

For many years I have been part of a small group of friends that meet once a month to simply talk about life, the universe, the world, ourselves, anything.

On occasion an activity is arranged where we meet some especially interesting person or organization. The group has many contacts around the world.

On one such occasion we visited the anthroposophical community in Järna south of Stockholm. This is a rare and admirable enclave of people who look at life and nature a little differently to the rest of us. And they walk their talk. They have created one of Europe's largest coherent areas of biodynamic agriculture, they run sophisticated educational programmes in art and agriculture, they have a hospital where patients are reviewed and treated as whole persons, not just for their ulcer or broken leg, they have homes for gravely disturbed children, and many other things. What the anthroposophists have created in Järna is something quite unique and interesting. If you are worried about where our civilization is headed, here you can find a living example that positive options actually exist.

We sat in a beautiful room with an open fire in the very special, newly built cultural centre. It sits on a large field like a shimmering, bluish vision from another world. The chairman of the Anthroposophical Society, Anders Kumlander, had just told us about the various activities and we were duly impressed.

After the meeting he came up to me. I asked later him why he chose me in particular but he didn't know, it was just a feeling. "Would you like to see our new concert hall here in the building?" he asked.

Sure I would, and we walked down a wide staircase and into a corridor. Anders opened a big door and suddenly we were standing in a magnificent concert hall with room for about four hundred people. We walked up on to the stage. The December dusk, filtering in through coloured glass windows, prompted Anders to go behind the scenes and turn on the lights. I stood at the front of the stage and became almost enchanted when the hall was lit up. The whole ceiling was one big piece of art; the walls were made of 12-centimetre-thick handcrafted planks of fir.

Anders came out from behind the curtains and I said: "What a fantastic concert hall. The acoustics here must be great."

"Yes, they are very good," said Anders, "most musicians love to play here. There is only one thing we lack right now – a concert grand piano."

I was startled. "There may be a solution to that problem," I said, and tried to stay calm enough to tell him about my big grand piano, which ought to find a more suitable home. Anders was very interested.

"The situation now," he said, "is that we actually have a small Steinway, an A-model, but it has proved too small for this hall."

"There is probably a solution to that too," I said, hardly able to believe what had just transpired.

A few days later I was back in the cultural centre for a meeting with Peter deVoto, who was the manager for the activities in the house. Over lunch we were to discuss the details of the grand piano switch. During our conversation I happened to mention our plans to build a new house on the plot that I had so luckily found. Peter was curious and asked where this plot was situated. I tried to explain, which was not so easy since it was in a small enclave with just a few houses that were visible only from the seaside. The place was pretty unknown, even to people who lived on the island.

"Oh, that place," said Peter, "I know it very well. I have walked across it a thousand times. You see, I was brought up in the house next door."

How strange. What a coincidence. Naturally, I then told him about my plans for the garden and happened to mention my difficulties in finding that nice gardener I had seen on television, Krantz, or whatever his name was.

"Oh, Lars," said Peter, "he is an old friend of mine. I can help you get in touch with him."

Once again I was startled. I felt as if I were floating along on a river that was headed in just the right direction. Peter asked what kind of a house we were about to build. I told him about our ideas and happened to mention the problems with the architect, which were a bit hard to define. They were not very clear, and I really had nothing bad to say about the man. It was just a feeling.

"I know an architect here in Järna," said Peter. "We have consulted him a couple of times and I think he is quite good. I am driving past the place where he works after lunch, so if you want you could come along and I will introduce him to you."

Sure, why not. I felt I needed all the contacts and impressions I could get at this stage.

We drove off and arrived eventually at a big, old, almost ramshackle house situated next to a cemetery. The house has been renovated now, but then it definitely did not look like the home of an architectural firm. Neither the squeaky old wooden staircase up to the second floor nor the office itself was a very good advertisement for it. I have seen a few architectural offices in my time. They are as a rule exquisitely designed, often very modern, even extreme sometimes. The architects themselves are usually dressed in a relaxed style with clothes of the highest quality and well-matched colours.

The only way to describe the office of Prisma Architects is that it was the exact opposite. I decided not to immediately judge what I saw. Out through a door came a tall bearded figure who looked as if he had just walked in from the woods. Peter introduced us. We shook hands and I heard myself say: "Would you like to help us build a house?"

"Sure, why not?" said the big bearded man.

What had I said? What had I done? I did not know him, I had never even met him, I had not seen anything he had done and I did not even know whether he was a bona fide architect. I had not discussed the matter with Catherine, it had popped up just half an hour ago, and there was nothing about him or the office to indicate that he would be the right person to design our nice new house.

So said the intellect. But for once the intuition had been faster.

A very fruitful cooperation started up in that messy office. Walter Druml came from Austria and had a solid architectural education. At some point in his life he had decided on a more anthroposophical lifestyle, and was quite uninterested in any rules that might spell out what an architect should look like.

He came out to our plot, which we had now begun to call Bäckastrand. He spent hours just watching the light, sitting on stones and looking around. He walked about in the grass and over the rounded rocks, peered up into the treetops, measured and paced, sucked in the atmosphere and the desires of the place.

It was surely not an easy task to combine them with our more or less wild fantasies about the new house. But Walter was patient. He calmly explained why certain things were impossible and instead presented other ideas and solutions that we had never thought of. When Catherine and I had different opinions and tension built up, which happened not so rarely, he waited patiently, slightly amused, for the energy to peter out. We never managed to make him side with one of us or the other.

With a certain anguish I had to pay the bill and say thank you and goodbye to the first architect. It was especially difficult since I did not have any rational or logical reason, and he was a generally nice and sympathetic person. But there is no doubt that Walter was absolutely the right man for the project. We now have lived for some years at Bäckastrand and every day I try to remember to send a grateful thought to the universe for the privilege of living in a home that we love.

In one single sweep of related synchronicities, the piano

problem, the garden adviser problem and the architect problem had found their solutions.

The house was nominated for the "Träpriset" (Wood Award – a special prize instituted by the Swedish Forest Industries Federation and presented every four years). It was also nominated for a local award, "The most liked house in Lidingö".

23 Can you evoke synchronicities?

The frequency of the occurrence of meaningful coincidences seems to increase with meditation.

Frank Joseph

If you wear mathematical and statistical spectacles, it is probably pretty obvious that coincidences are not something that you can evoke or influence. But if you replace them with a pair of holistic, multidimensional spectacles, a lot of things become possible.

Many who have studied the question seem to lean towards the opinion that synchronistic events become more frequent when people practise meditation, yoga, relaxation, qigong or any other form of training that enhances the focusing of consciousness.

Personally, I learned transcendental meditation in 1971 and have since tried and practised various techniques. I've not always been disciplined and regular, but some form of meditation has somehow always been present in my life ever since.

The following piece is borrowed from Peter Russell's home page, "The spirit of now" (www.peterrussell.com). I highly recommend a visit to this magical and insightful website. Peter has an unusual combination in his academic background: mathematics, computer science and psychology. He is a highly sought-after author and lecturer all around the world, and among other things he has published the fascinating books *From Science to God* and *The White Hole in Time*.

I really wanted to incorporate Peter's text in this book, since it gives a brilliant insight into the mystery – and simplicity – of synchronicity. Peter kindly gave his permission to reproduce it.

How to be a wizard
by Peter Russell

A wizard knows the laws of creation, and how to work with them.

A wizard allows synchronicity to manifest.

A wizard follows three basic principles.

The first principle is that of wholeness. The more rested I am, the more relaxed my mind and body, the more in touch I am with my self, the more free I feel, the easier my soul, the more whole I am. And the more whole I am, the more synchronicity seems to occur.

Conversely, when I am out of balance, tired, stressed, frazzled, wrapped up in concern or in some other way off center, synchronicity does not manifest nearly so abundantly.

We cannot make synchronicities happen. It is in their very nature to occur "by coincidence". We cannot control or manipulate the world in order to create synchronicities – their source is not of this world. Yet we can encourage their appearance; we can open ourselves to them. This we do by opening to ourselves, to our inner wholeness.

A wizard allows inner wholeness to be a priority. A wizard keeps rested, relaxed, centered and clear.

A second characteristic of synchronicities is that they tend to support our needs. They seem to bring us just what we need, at just the right time. It is as if the Universe has my best interests at heart, and arranges for their fulfilment in ways which I could never have dreamt of. It is, to quote a renowned Indian teacher, "the support of nature". We support nature by centering ourselves, and nature supports us back, providing the opportunities to fulfil our needs. This is what makes them so magical and remarkable – such a coincidence.

To allow the support of nature into our lives we need to follow the second principle of wizardry – intuition. This can be hard, because it is often difficult to know what is true intuition and what is just "stuff" seeping up from our unconscious. For me, following my intuition means following my feelings, not my thoughts.

A good example occurred one afternoon in May 1995. I was busy writing when suddenly I had the inclination to get up and go for a walk. At first I resisted – I told myself I was meant to be working. Then, when the feeling persisted, I got up and went for what I term a "random walk" – I don´t decide in advance where I am going; at each point where I have a choice, I make my choice there and then.

As I walked I noticed signs for an artist's open day. The third time I saw the sign I decided to follow it. Wandering around the studio, looking at some wonderful sculptures, I happened to notice a guy in another room, working away on a Macintosh. I wandered in and found he was developing a web server, and wanted to do very much the same thing as myself. We found we had many other interests in common, and instantly became very good friends. He offered me a place for my own web site, and a few weeks later I had my first pages up and running.

That is an example of following my intuition. If I had got on with what I thought I should be doing, we might never have met. Many things would have turned out differently, and you might not be reading this now.

It is as if cosmic choreography has already set up the coincidences. They are there waiting for us to discover them. We pick up the possibilities through some subtle mental antenna, and notice them as some vague tickling of our attention – an intuition.

And there is one more principle I have discovered. I can sit alone in my cottage in the middle of a forest, at peace in myself, centered and whole, and in touch with my intuition, yet here few coincidences occur. Significant coincidences nearly always seem to involve other people in some way. It is as if our interplay with others gives cosmic choreography greater opportunities to reach through to us.

Although we may not be able to make synchronicities happen, we can create an inner environment of wholeness and an openness to intention; and in our outer lives we can go and engage ourselves fully in the world, mix with the social field, go out and play. Play whatever game and role best fits our intuitions. Play it with our soul, fully. Play it in whatever way brings us inner wholeness, enjoyment and fulfilment – there is, after all, no point in suffering while we play.

This is the third principle of wizardry – a principle I call "zipping and zooming". Playing our part in the world, and allowing cosmic choreography to play its part.

These are the three principles of wizardry: Wholeness, Intuition, and Zipping and Zooming.

And if you need a mnemonic to remember them by, simply take their initial letters, W I Z – a wizard wizzes.

24 *The right colour*

We had just held the topping-out party at Bäckastrand. The construction began looking more and more like a house, but still there were many decisions to be made. Building a new house is to face a constant barrage of new questions. Regardless of how carefully you have planned, things always pop up that nobody had thought of or anticipated. How wide should this strip of wood be? Do we use plywood here? How do you want this joint? Every day there are new decisions to be made.

One question that had become urgent was the colour of the indoor walls. We knew we wanted something calm. We wanted to reflect the harmony and quietude of the place. No strong colours. One source of inspiration was pictures of Japanese interiors with quiet grey and beige nuances.

After much discussion with the painters we decided that the wooden parts should be grey. But I had never understood how many different hues exist that could be called grey. It seems to be a colour that dances well with just about any other colour, and changes like a chameleon depending on its dancing partner. Yellow, red, blue, green, white, black, violet; the grey colour lacks a strong self-identity and is easily influenced in any direction. It was a great relief when we at last reached a decision about the right hue of grey.

Now all we had to decide was the beige wall colour. This was even more difficult, as we discovered that beige has even more hues than grey. In spite of now having the grey colour to base a decision on, the endless flipping through tiny colour samples became increasingly confusing. This was such an important choice. Our anxiety grew with the stacks of colour samples.

Finally we gave up and went to the Scandinavian Colour Institute. Maybe we could get some help there. At least they had large binders with big and clear colour samples. We had brought a little piece of wood painted with the right grey colour, so as to make it easier to find the perfect combination.

We sat at a table browsing through three binders full of only beige hues. This one might be good ... or this one ... no, this one ... why not this ... or ... our sense of colour began evaporating. My head was a disorganized mess of beige. But we had to make a choice. The binders just lay there open and waiting for us to decide. We looked desperately at each other. What the hell should we do?

Suddenly there was a hand hovering over the table. A finger pointed at one of the samples and a voice said: "That one is very nice."

We looked up and saw a friendly lady, who had materialized at our table without us noticing. She went on: "That one you can combine with these three hues." She flipped through the binder with a deft hand and showed some other samples. "With this, this one and that one. They are all in the same colour scale but have different brightness. Paint the darkest rooms with the lightest hues and then gradually with the darker hues the brighter the room is. These four hues work perfectly together and they will give your house a nice balance in combination with the grey you have there on that piece of wood."

Our jaws just fell open. It was totally unexpected. Who was she? Where did she come from? How did she know all this?

"Write down the numbers on the samples so you get the exact colours. Oh, I have to go. I am a colour consultant and I'm just teaching a course in there," she pointed to a door, "but the break is over now so I must go back. Your home will look very nice. Good luck with the painting!"

She disappeared as quickly as she had appeared.

We went home and did exactly as she had said. It looks pretty good.

25 *The floor man*

The stairs to the second floor of our newly built house were made from oak that had to be sanded and oiled. The sanding was done but the oiling had been deferred with all the other small jobs that were yet to be done. Time passes and you get used to things being as they are.

But suddenly one day something catches your eye; you see the unfinished stuff anew and think: No, this can't go on! It's time take action!

I tried to remember the name of that floor man who had promised to oil the stairs. He was a nice young man who, together with a colleague, had built, sanded and oiled all the oak floors in the house. He had agreed also to treat the surface of the stairs, but somehow the whole thing had been forgotten.

Now, damn it, it's about time! I began looking for his name and phone number among the binders and piles of papers left over from the building project. What was his name again? It had totally disappeared from my memory, which did not help my search. I found nothing, but had a vague notion of the name of the company he worked for. I looked through the phone book and felt pretty smug when it seemed that my memory was still intact. I found the company name I thought I remembered, and dialled the number, feeling relief that I would now get hold of the guy and finally get the stairs fixed.

The number was discontinued. There was no information regarding any new number, nothing. I was back to square one. But had he not given us a calling card? It must be here somewhere. More searching through stacks of calling cards. No luck. Nothing in our private phone book. Nothing hiding in some forgotten pile of papers on the desk. Not even Catherine, who is good at keeping track of things, could remember or find anything. But we must get the darn stairs finished! Who can do it instead? Who does that kind of work? The questions nagged us.

I had to quit searching for the time being since I was due to attend a jazz luncheon with the Swedish Executive Jazz Society. It is a nice Friday tradition where you eat, listen and perhaps participate in a jam session.

When I arrived there were a couple of hundred people in the ballroom, and it seemed pretty crowded around the tables. I was late because of my search for the floor man. I looked around the room, trying to spot a free chair, but it seemed hopeless. Then I caught a glimpse of my musician friend Dick Nilson in a corner across the room. He waved at me and I waved back. He pointed emphatically down at the table and I understood that there was actually an empty chair at his very table. What luck! I criss-crossed the room, happy to find somewhere to sit. It was probably the only free chair left in the place.

I said hello to Dick and the guy sitting to my right. I vaguely recognized him. We had met at some earlier event, but I could not immediately remember who he was. He introduced himself and now I remembered that he was an architect.

He obviously knew that we had built a new house and asked

about the building process and how we had found it. I told him a little about how much we loved the house, but I could not help whining a bit over the mystery of the floor guy who had disappeared from sight, since it was so fresh in my mind.

"Oh, you mean Peter, Peter Berggren, the man who laid the floor in your house. He works with me now. I have his phone number here if you want to reach him."

That I did. A week later Peter had finished the stairs.

26 Project Stargate

The unconscious of a falling stone is something totally different from the unconscious of a growing cabbage.

Henri Bergson

Dale Graff was a physicist at the US Air Force Foreign Technology Division in the 1970s. He had a reasonably comfortable existence, well anchored in the materialistic world view. His job was to analyse and report on technological advances in various areas, and also to predict future technological developments. But here he was nagged by an irritating problem. It was almost impossible to predict anything more than a couple of years ahead. Political, economical and social factors could at any moment change the projected future. Not to speak of the human factor, the sudden stroke of genius, the unexpected breakthrough, and all the unpredictable psychological aspects.

The most irritating and difficult element of all was the science being researched rather intensively in the Soviet Union, focusing on what was called "bioenergy". In the West it was called ESP, extrasensory perception, or *psi*, a Greek letter used to make exceptional human abilities appear a little more neutral and less mystical. The Soviet scientists studied things like telepathy, psychokinesis (the ability to influence material objects with pure power of thought) and other so-called "paranormal phenomena". Among other things they carried out experiments studying telepathic communication with submarines at sea. They called it "transmission of emotions". Several of the Soviet cosmonauts were also interested and engaged in the work on bioenergy. This, of course, worried the American military leadership.

Even if many viewed this as an utterly suspect area of science, it was decided that the Americans had to begin studying it a bit more closely. Dale Graff was made chief of this super-secret project, and was given a new position at DIA, the Defence Intelligence Agency. What happened there was to change his life.

He named the project "Stargate" and worked closely with the nuclear physicists Hal Puthoff and Russell Targ at the Stanford Research Institute. They were doing research into something called "remote viewing" (more on that in the chapter about intuition, on page 174). What Graff discovered changed his whole world view, and in his book *Tracks in the Psychic Wilderness* he tells as much as he can without revealing those parts that are classified.

It is enough to raise several eyebrows.

He discovered that it was totally possible for a psi-gifted person to sit in the laboratory and, through nothing other than his own inner pictures, quite correctly describe a secret military base in the Soviet Union that at the time was totally unknown.

One of the test subjects, Pat Price, described, for instance, buildings and dome-shaped structures that nobody had seen or heard of, and the scientists could not understand what they had been built for. It was not until after the fall of the Soviet Union that it was verified that the base and those structures actually existed exactly as Price had described them.

During the work Graff also had reason to study and contemplate synchronistic events. He arrived at the conclusion that they occur through something more than pure, mathematical chance. He writes: "Synchronicities are dynamic events that occur at surprising times in response to pressing needs or concerns. Synchronistic experiences remind us there is much we do not yet understand about the reach of our conscious and subconscious mind."

He sought explanations in something called *non-local quantum effects*, and mentioned, for example, a strange discovery in quantum physics. Two elementary particles that have been connected to each other may be separated by hundreds of miles. And if you change the rotation of one of them the other will change in exactly the same way at exactly the same moment, regardless of the distance between them. This is called *quantum synchronicity* or *non-locality*, and there are no known laws of cause and effect which can explain it. Graff says that there continues to exist a meaningful connection between the particles in some kind of holistic relationship that is not bound by the limitations of time and space. "Synchronistic events toss hints of how our subconscious mind may operate and suggest that aspects of our brain and deep layers of our psyche may be wavelike in nature, similar to the manner in which a hologram functions."

It may not be so easy to grasp, but it does feel like another little piece of the synchronicity puzzle.

27 *The concrete man*

On 29 September 1994 the ferry *Estonia* capsized in the Baltic Sea; 852 people died in this horrible accident.

I was astonished at how clumsy the Swedish authorities were in handling the *Estonia* catastrophe. That clumsiness has turned *Estonia* into a constantly bleeding wound that will not heal. Associations of relatives now and then air their anger and frustration, maritime experts disagree, conspiracy theoreticians are delving to find the truth, the media do not know which leg to stand on, and the authorities seem to send out smokescreens trying to put a lid on the whole affair.

The first reaction to this terrible accident was sound and normal. Both the prime minister and the opposition leader at the time said that everything would be done to salvage the ship and its tragic cargo of dead bodies as soon as possible.

Why didn't they?

It would have been an unpleasant period with horrible images, much grief, many burials and black headlines. But then it would have been over. Most relatives of the deceased would have had definite confirmation, closure – a coffin, a burial site to go to, so that the grief and the shock could eventually subside and leave room for brighter memories of the deceased.

Now they have not been given that opportunity. Why did

the ship sink? Where is my husband? How did my daughter die? What actually happened? Lots of questions are still hovering unanswered, and therefore the wounds will not heal.

It is a known psychological fact that the human organism has an innate need to finish things. Unfinished traumatic experiences gather like stones in our inner rucksack from early childhood.

A little boy shows his father a drawing he has made of a car. The father, knowing that it is good to encourage the creativity of children, heaps praise on the proud little boy. The next day the boy sees an opportunity to get even more praise and make his father even happier. He takes his crayon and draws a giant car on the white wall of the living room.

The father comes home and goes ballistic. The boy is shocked and scared and cannot understand. Dad was so happy about the little car yesterday; why is he so angry about the big one today? But the boy cannot express his confusion and distress, and the whole incident is turned into a big rock in his inner rucksack.

We gather our rocks, big and small, along our life's path, and eventually we may get more and more bent from our heavier and heavier rucksack. Many of the experiences and feelings hide in those rocks we have repressed, pulling a veil of forgetfulness over them in order to avoid the pain. But the charges are still there, ready to pop up in a sudden burst of emotion, perhaps activated by something happening here and now that has absolutely nothing to do with what happened there and then.

In therapy language it is often called "unfinished business" or "introjections", like inner packs of energy ready to burst open at any time if activated. It could even make us do something we might regret.

Perhaps the boy grows up and becomes a bona fide graffiti artist. Or, the reverse, feels an unreasonable hatred for everything that has to do with graffiti, maybe even becomes violent if he catches sight of someone spraying graffiti. In both cases he might find himself in trouble here and now for something that happened when he was four years old, and which he has long ago forgotten. Psychotherapy is partially about finding those rocks, taking them out of the rucksack and throwing them by the roadside to give us a lighter step on the walk of life.

I wonder how many debilitating inner rocks the *Estonia* affair has created in thousands of relatives? And what chances do they have to get rid them? The charges are noticeable in the constant conflicts that pop up, but seem to lead nowhere. The authorities do all they can to repress, deny and pretend that everything is as it should be. But the *Estonia* lies there in the depths of the Baltic Sea with her dark secrets; a gigantic example of "unfinished business".

One of the most preposterous ideas that was put forth, and for which preliminary work had actually started, was to pour concrete over the whole ship. A mountain of concrete at the bottom of the sea would forever hide what had happened. Perhaps the hope was also that the sorrow and the loss might disappear into the interior of the gigantic concrete tombstone down there in the cold darkness. And no one would ever be able to find any proof or evidence of any wrongdoing, mistakes or criminal negligence. Everything would be hidden, forever repressed and forgotten.

I disliked the idea immensely and did not think that the thousands of relatives would feel better if this whole catastrophe were repressed and hidden under an immense concrete sarcophagus at the bottom of the sea. It seemed like a magnificent manifestation of stupidity and denial.

I was reminded of the *Estonia* during a lecture at the Swedish Institute of Management, where I was leading a two-day seminar on leadership and personal development. The participants were 25 architects and engineers from various companies within the Sweco group of building and construction consultants. I was talking about the need to finish things, and how all the troubles relating to the *Estonia* illustrated what happens when you don't. I vented my dismay over the authorities' clumsy handling of the affair, and especially the preposterous idea of pouring concrete over it all.

A somewhat strange atmosphere in the room caught my attention. It suddenly struck me that here I was, standing in a room full of construction people, and speaking ill of a big construction project. What if someone in the room was involved? I felt a "disturbance in the field", as Darth Vader would have said, and became unsure of what to do. I decided I might as well grab the bull by the horns.

"Here I am standing talking about something that you probably know a lot more about than I do. Maybe there is even someone here who is working with that project?"

At that exact moment the door opened and a man became visible in the door opening.

"There he is," several voices said simultaneously.

There was mumbling and a bit of laughter in the room. What were they talking about? What was happening? The man had been gone only a couple of hours, called away on some urgent business matter. He stopped and looked inquisitively at me, as confused as I was.

Then several cheerful voices informed me; the man at the door was the very person who was heading the whole project of burying the *Estonia* under a mountain of concrete!

There was some stirring in the room over the strange fact

that he had popped up at exactly the same moment as I had asked whether anyone there was involved. He then went on to tell us that the whole project had been stopped. That was the reason he had been called away for a while.

He did not seem particularly distressed. Nor did anyone else. Quite a few of them had actually thought that it was a pretty strange assignment. Big and unique, for sure, and probably very profitable for the concrete business, but strange.

I got out of the situation without a bloody nose, but with the intention of being a little more careful the next time I was about to criticize something in public.

28 *The bass players' world*

Every world has its heroes and role models. In the world of football, for instance, stars like Ronaldo, Zlatan and Beckham are adored by millions of fans. The world of science looks up to its Nobel Prize winners, and honours trailblazers like Rupert Sheldrake, Bruce Lipton and Karl Pribram. In the world of rock music there is a bigger crowd of gods than on the Greek Olympus.

The world of jazz too has its household gods. One of them was the bass player Ray Brown, a hero to generations of jazz musicians. Not least to Hans Backenroth, one of Sweden's finest and most sought-after young bass players. I must confess, as an amateur bassist, that Hans himself is one of my favourites. As is, of course, Ray Brown.

Hans had a gig in Iceland together with the clarinet player Putte Wickman. They were due to return home early in the morning and took a taxi to Reykjavik airport. It was still dark outside when they got near the airport and they could see the lights from an airliner approaching the runway.

Suddenly the taxi driver pointed at the aircraft and said: "Here comes Mr Ray Brown."

Hans thought it funny that a taxi driver in Iceland should happen to mention the name of one of his personal heroes and asked what he meant.

It was simply that the driver had been pre-booked to pick Mr Brown up at the airport. He also knew that Brown was to give a concert in Reykjavik.

Inside the terminal Hans strolled around in the duty-free shop with his bow case under his arm. He was overjoyed when he found a couple of CDs featuring the Oscar Peterson trio for which he had been looking for a long time. And who was the bass player on both of them? Ray Brown, of course. Nice coincidence, Hans thought.

He paid the cashier and was just on his way out of the shop when his mobile phone rang. "Hi, it's Kjell." It was the piano player Kjell Öhman, who was calling from a city in Sweden. He was on tour with the singer Alice Babs.

"Can you help me? We are going to play that song 'Love You Madly' and I didn't bring the music. There is a hell of a good bass line introduction in there that Ray Brown played, do you know it?"

Hans laughed. "How cool. This is the third time in the last half-hour that Ray Brown has popped up. First the cab driver said here comes Ray Brown when we saw a plane, and then I bought two Oscar Peterson CDs with Ray Brown on bass, and now you call asking about a Ray Brown bass part. Pretty strange."

At the same moment Hans felt someone touching his arm and heard a voice saying "Hello". He turned around, and there stood … Ray Brown.

Just as I had finished writing this chapter, I closed down Microsoft Word to go on the Internet. Ray Brown was still on my mind. My starting page with CNN News came up, and my eyes were immediately drawn to a headline that made my hair stand on end.

"Ray Brown is dead."

He had been on tour in the USA and was to give a concert in the evening. It was getting close to starting time and the other musicians were in place, but there was no sign of Ray. He always used to be on time. They began to wonder. They knew that a few hours earlier he had gone to his room to rest for a while. Maybe he's overslept, they thought, and went off to wake him.

Ray Brown would never wake up again. He was seventy-five years old. The jazz world, and especially the bass players' world, had lost one of its big heroes.

29 What do we know?

> *Physics is mathematical, not because we know so*
> *much about the physical world, but because we know*
> *so little; it is only its mathematical properties we can*
> *discover.*

Bertrand Russell

As far as I know there is no research anywhere in the world focusing specifically on the phenomenon of synchronicity. But many researchers are interested in it and there are some speculations and theories. Some actual research projects also appear to be nibbling at the edge of the phenomenon.

The central questions seem to be: Is there a field of consciousness that is not simply trapped inside the skull of man? Maybe not even limited to space and time. And if there is such a field, could it somehow influence what happens in matter–time–space? And if so, could it imply the beginning of a deeper understanding of what synchronicity is?

There seem to be two main trains of thought when looking at synchronicity. That is perhaps true of our world view in general. One sticks to the old habitual paradigm, the materialistic, positivistic, reductionistic world view, which does not want to know of any reality beyond that which can be measured and weighed and calculated, touched and controlled. Synchronicities are seen simply as a matter of statistics and mathematics. Chances and probabilities are calculated with advanced, and to me very impressive, mathematical models and reasoning. One juggles with concepts like *bionominal coefficients, stochastic variables* and *combinatorics*. One can calculate *probability amplitudes* and predict how many people are celebrating their birthday in a concert audience of 10,000, or the probability that heads will come up between 40 and 60 times if you flip a coin 100 times – an average of 50 times exactly. I have not chosen these simple examples in order to belittle statistical mathematics. I choose them because they are simple enough for me to understand.

An advanced knowledge of statistics and mathematics is very important in many different areas – for example, computer science and social planning. And I think that it could even be of great value in research about synchronicity, if those who have mastered it could bring themselves to approach the subject seriously.

But the mathematical model can never get a grip on the emotional, psychological contents of an event. It is brilliant at handling the objective, but helpless when it comes to the subjective. Mathematics simply does not like that.

In his learned book *True or Probable*, the professor of mathematical statistics Allan Gut writes a little condescendingly: "It can be worth adding that there are people who wish to interpret supposed unexplainable coincidences as a sign from above, as determined by fate."

Yes, there are people like that. And how can one be sure that there is no merit in their interpretations? They represent the other train of thought about synchronicity, an attitude that seems to attract more and more laymen as well as scholars. Those who sometimes wonder deeply about reality, what it is all about, and at least remain open about the question: Is there perhaps an "above" from which we could actually receive "signs"?

Personally I do not believe that everything in life is determined by fate. I do not think that a person's life is a predetermined path marked out by paper strips, or like a trip on the Phantom Manor Ride at Disneyland, where everything that happens is arranged beforehand. I believe in man's free will and personal responsibility. And I know that every psychologically healthy person can to a large degree influence how his or her life develops.

But I suspect that for most people this takes place in some kind of unconscious interplay with the "above", this collective, or even cosmic, consciousness, or field of information and energy, or universe, or God, or whatever we prefer to call it. It is certainly something. And piece after piece of the puzzle is being found, even if the big picture is still far from complete.

30 *The actor and the murderer*

Edwin Booth was one of America's first world-famous actors. He was very popular and admired, especially for his interpretations of Shakespeare. He was also feted in Europe, having played both Hamlet and Macbeth on several European stages. This was in the 1800s, long before the Hollywood era. Today he would have been a megastar, constantly appearing on talk shows and in gossip magazines.

But one day something happened that made him instantly disappear from the stage. He suddenly received a devastating message. President Abraham Lincoln had been murdered. That was bad enough. But even worse; the name of the murderer was John Wilkes Booth.

The murderer was Edwin's own brother.

Edwin was stunned and totally broke down. He could no longer go on stage. He sank into a gloomy and depressive existence. His life became progressively more and more miserable, and his once-so-enthusiastic following began to forget about him.

A few wretched years had passed when one day he stood waiting for the train on a crowded platform at a station in New Jersey. Suddenly there was a scream near by. He saw a well-dressed young man falling down on to the tracks, probably shoved by the crowd. A train was rapidly approaching.

Edwin reacted instinctively. He pushed forward, and holding on with one hand to a piece of railing, he stretched down to grab the young man. He managed to get hold of him and pull him back up on the platform unharmed. Booth was very close to getting hit by the train himself.

A short time thereafter he received a letter from the famous general Ulysses S. Grant. That letter made Edwin get his existence back in order, and enabled him to return to the stage and his life as an actor. As long as he lived he constantly carried the letter with him in his pocket.

In the letter General Grant thanked him, and also conveyed the gratitude of the man's mother, for having saved the life of Robert Todd Lincoln.

Robert was the son of Mary and Abraham Lincoln.

Edwin Booth had saved the life of the son of the man his brother had killed.

31 *The postcard man*

The late piano player Charlie Norman is one of the legends of Swedish jazz history. Just a few months before he passed away he told me the following story with a voice still full of laughter.

In 1956 Charlie was in Honolulu with his band. They were performing with the American vocal group the Delta Rhythm Boys, who had become extremely popular in Sweden, having toured the country several times. Their versions of old Swedish folk songs in broken Swedish particularly still live in the memories of many older people.

Television was a new invention at the time, existing only in a few homes, and on Saturday evenings neighbours often gathered at the lucky owner's house to behold this miracle. There was just one channel transmitting in black and white for a few hours every evening.

Charlie Norman and his group often accompanied the handsome gentlemen in the Delta Rhythm Boys. They were frequent guests on television and became extremely popular with the Swedish public, at the time still pretty homogeneous and perhaps a bit isolated. My father was a great fan. He had himself been singing with a barber shop quartet and admired the way they used their voices.

Charlie was himself one of my early favourites in the jazz

world. He introduced the boogie-woogie into Sweden and really rubbed the cultural puritans the wrong way with his boogie-woogie version of Grieg's 'Anitra's Dance'. I loved it, and tried frantically to learn how to play it on the piano. I was not very successful.

Charlie also hosted one of the few weekly jazz programmes on the one and only radio channel. It was probably the first real disc jockey programme on Swedish radio – the format in which someone just chats to the listeners and plays records. He was also very humorous and played just the right kind of music in the opinion of us schoolboys, even if many grown-ups frowned at this "noise". We sat glued to the radio on those sacred evenings when his programme *The Night Owl* was on.

Now Charlie Norman's cooperation with the Delta Rhythm Boys had led to a tour that took them all the way to Honolulu. It was long before the era of charter travel. The Swedes had not yet become a travelling people, blasé and at home in most parts of the world. Few had ever been to Honolulu.

For a Swedish jazz group this was an unusual and enviable mission, so Charlie and his musicians wanted to send some postcards to family and friends at home. They felt that it was the least they could do, being on the other side of the globe, having a lot of fun in the sun.

They found a small shop with racks of postcards. A friendly little Chinese man stood behind the counter, and when he heard them speaking a foreign language he asked where they came from.

"From Sweden," they answered. In those days it was common for people abroad not to know very much about this little country in a remote corner of the world. You were quite likely to receive a comment like "You make good watches". It wasn't so easy to know the difference between Sweden and Switzerland.

"Oh, from Sweden!" he cried out. To their surprise he became totally excited and ran into a small room behind the counter. Hey, this little guy knows about Sweden, they thought almost proudly. When he came back he was frantically waving two records, the old stiff kind, since the LP had not quite made it to the market yet.

"I must show you something," he hollered.

It turned out that he was a great jazz enthusiast and collector of records. The two records he had brought out were Swedish recordings with Lars Gullin, the baritone saxophone player and composer, one of the greatest icons of Swedish jazz music. The Chinese man was extremely knowledgeable and bubbled on profusely about the exquisite music created by Lars Gullin.

He put one of the records on the record player. He was particularly enthusiastic over the fantastic guitar player who played with Gullin. When a guitar solo came up the Chinese man stared mesmerized at the record player and cried: "He is incredible, he is fabulous! Just listen!" He moved in rhythm with the playing, closed his eyes and sank into the glory of the music. It was as if he were in direct contact with the divine. "Listen to this!" he screamed when there were some particularly fine phrases. "Listen! Oh, isn't he wonderful! His name is Rolf Berg. Have you heard of him?"

They all giggled and Charlie pointed.

"He is standing right there."

Rolf Berg was one of the members of Charlie's group.

The Chinese man gaped. He looked as if he was beginning to faint. Then he collected himself, rushed around the counter and hugged Rolf Berg with tears in his eyes, shouting: "It's God´s hand! It's God´s hand!"

Well, at least it was a nice little piece of synchronicity.

Charlie also told me of another funny episode that he had

heard about from the orchestra leader and conductor Gunnar Lundén-Welden. It happened in the 1930s when Lundén-Welden was on tour with his orchestra in western Sweden. He was driving the tour bus himself and had five musicians as passengers. There were mainly dirt roads in those days, and you still drove on the left.

Suddenly the bus came too close to the verge and the left wheels began to skid in the gravel. A few long and distressed seconds passed as the bus seemed to lose its footing. They were all horrified, thinking that the bus would turn over.

Somehow Lundén-Welden eventually managed to avoid the ditch and get the vehicle back up on the road again. There was total silence in the bus. Nobody said "Shit, that was close" or "Damn, I got scared!" or "What kind of crap driving was that?" Nobody moaned or sighed or whimpered from relief. Everybody was absolutely silent.

Suddenly, at exactly the same moment and in exactly the same key, all five musicians began to sing "If you knew Susie, like I know Susie".

Nobody could explain why.

32 Morphic fields

If an idea does not seem bizarre to begin with, it is nothing to hope for.

Niels Bohr

Rupert Sheldrake, a British biochemist and cell biologist, has introduced a theory of something called *morphic fields*. It seems to be gaining increasing interest. He says that every individual consciousness is a field of energy that is connected to the brain but reaches far beyond it. Together the energy fields of people form a collective, greater field that he calls a *morphogenetic field*. (From the Greek word *morphe* = form, and *genesis* = to come into being.)

Each species of life has its own specific morphogenetic field. Our poodle has its dog field, the big oak by the gate has its oak field and the mosquito that bit me last summer has its mosquito field.

When Sheldrake was a researcher at Cambridge University, studying the development of plants, he became convinced that everything living is organized by energy fields. How can a minuscule embryo within a seed grow into a pine tree, or a

134

daisy, or a raspberry bush? What is it that give leafs, flowers and fruits their specific form?

The materialistic explanation is that the development of a plant, an animal or a human simply follows the instructions that are programmed in its genes. But that is only part of the truth. The problem is that those instructions are mostly about how to put the various building blocks together in the right order. The genes see to it that amino acids create the right proteins at the right time in the right place. But how can that explain the shape of a rose or the structure of a porcupine? How can it explain that you are you?

A house does not become a house just because the building workers put together boards and concrete in the right order. There must be an idea, information, about the shape and look of the house and how it is supposed to function. There must be an architectural drawing.

The morphogenetic field is that drawing. It has the information that determined how the fertilized egg should develop into that which is you today. Your field held the information necessary not only for the genes to start the construction work but also to tell them *how* they should do it to create that specific and unique being that is you. The drawing of you already existed in the greater human field. And it still does.

The atoms, the physical matter our bodies are made of, are said to be totally exchanged within two years. According to the physician and researcher Deepak Chopra, studies have been made with radio isotopes showing that the atoms in the lining of our stomachs are exchanged in five days, the liver takes five weeks, the bones three months, and so on. So we are not in fact the mobile statue we may have seen ourselves as, but rather a river that has the same shape from day to day, but whose contents are never the same.

Used atoms leave us when we breathe out. Every out-breath contains an enormous number of used atoms. And new ones come in with our food and breath. What is it that then makes the new atoms end up in the right place, so that I recognize myself in the mirror every morning? (At least, most mornings!) It is the drawing, the field, my own personal *morphic field*, which is a part of the greater *morphogenetic* human field.

But it is not just our physical form that has its basic drawing in the field. Our consciousness is also part of it, according to Sheldrake: "Through attention and intentions our minds stretch out into the world beyond our bodies."

That our intentions should be able to influence the field becomes especially interesting in relation to synchronicity. Sheldrake indicates that our needs, wishes, desires, loves, hate objects, duties, ambitions and other emotionally charged things become intentions that vibrate in the field. Could it be that we consciously or unconsciously send out signals into the universe, into the field, and as a response the field sets up and organizes events that influence our lives, solve problems or point to solutions? In other words, synchronicities?

Sheldrake uses a simple form of life as a metaphor, an amoeba that consists of just one cell, *Amoebia proteus*. It got its name from the Greek god of the seas, Proteus, who could change his shape. That is exactly what this little amoeba does. It may, for instance, live in a dam, where it eats bacteria. Moving around in search of something nice for lunch, it constantly changes its shape. Its body can bulge out on one side and be pulled in at the other. It can stretch pretty far in any direction, and is sometimes round, sometimes long and narrow. The protrusions it sends out into the world around it are called *pseudopodia*, also from the Greek language, meaning *false feet*.

The white blood cells in our immune system function in exactly the same way. They float around on patrol in our circulating blood, looking for bacteria or other intruders that shouldn't be there. When they identify an enemy they change shape, embrace it and squeeze it with their whole body. Soon the intruder is no more.

There are even stranger examples of amoeba-like behaviour in our bodies. Some of our brain cells can reach out with enormously long pseudopodia in order to send signals and communicate with their surroundings. They are called *axons*. Nerve cells in the spinal marrow in particular can send out axons that are up to a metre in length. Not bad for a little cell that you can hardly see with the naked eye.

According to Sheldrake it is no accident that mind has its roots in the brain, which itself is a network of nerve cells with pseudopodia-like axons reaching out far beyond the cells. He speculates that mind works in the same way.

Our *intentions* become like *axons* of energy and information that are being sent out into the world, or rather into the field around us. There they are in a gigantic soup of other energy and information, and who knows what they can create out there? And who knows how that in turn might influence what happens in our lives, in matter, space and time?

Doesn't this look like yet another piece of the puzzle, a fragment of the big picture that eventually should reveal the true nature of synchronicity?

33 *"Basin Street Blues"*

I participated in a week-long jazz seminar on the beautiful island of Visingsö. The leader of my group was the great trombone player Bertil Strandberg. Among his credits can be mentioned four years with the famous Artie Shaw Big Band in the USA and several years with the German Radio Orchestra in Stuttgart.

We were rehearsing for a concert to be performed the same evening, and were just about to start working anew with the old standard "Basin Street Blues" in a newly written and modernized arrangement by Bertil.

We waited for Bertil to set the tempo. In the concentrated silence there was a sudden cry from the trumpet player, Arne Lingenstrand: "Where the hell are my sheets?" He flipped frantically through the papers on his music stand, supposed to hold the eight tunes we were to play at the concert. "I can't find 'Basin Street Blues'! Has anybody seen my sheets? Shit, they're gone!"

The echo of his voice had hardly died away when the door opened and the band's singer, Lena, entered the room.

Bertil jokingly asked her: "Have you seen Arne's sheets for 'Basin Street Blues'?" Everybody laughed.

Lena did not understand what was so funny. She looked

with a quizzical expression first at Bertil, then at some papers she was holding in her hand.

"Are they these?" she said, and showed them to Bertil. He looked and his eyebrows went up. "Yes, they are!"

Lena didn't understand the uproar in the band. She didn't know about Arne's predicament and that his salvation was exactly what she held in her hand. She didn't know that she had come through the door just seconds after he had shouted "Where the hell are my sheets?"

She looked at the laughing musicians, confused. "I didn´t know what they were. Somebody had found some sheets and gave them to me and said that they probably belonged to our group. I never looked at them."

What is the statistical probability of this happening?

A lot of various circumstances must wind their way through time and space to converge at this exact moment, thus creating a meaningful coincidence. Perhaps not a big life-changing event, but still pretty improbable, and an event that immediately solved a troublesome problem. Not just for the trumpet player but for the whole group. Without that little synchronicity we would not have been able to play "Basin Street Blues", into which we already had put considerable effort.

Synchronicities are not always related to big and important issues in life. Sometimes it can just be funny little things. The universe has humour.

But even a small, seemingly simple coincidence may prove to be the result of a pretty intricate set of circumstances that all have to connect in a certain way.

If you try to unwind and look closer at this little incident, you see how many different factors have to interplay. Let us call the moment when Lena enters the door Moment X. An exact moment in time that also becomes the central focal point in a spiderweb of different, separate events that are all necessary for the actual problem to find its solution. They must also be perfectly coordinated. Here are just a few of them:

1. Bertil decides to write a special arrangement of "Basin Street Blues" for the jazz group he is to lead during the seminar.

2. Of all the thousands of minutes available during the seminar week, he decides to rehearse it a few minutes before Moment X.

3. Through a web of causes and effects, Arne Lingenstrand has been selected to play the trumpet in Bertil Strandberg's group.

4. Another web of cause and effect makes him misplace his sheets somewhere in the campus area.

5. He discovers the loss seconds before Moment X.

6. A totally different set of causes and effects leads to another person, perhaps an hour before Moment X, finding some sheets of music lying about somewhere. She picks them up and sees that they are "Basin Street Blues".

7. The person has for some reason, through yet another web of causes and effects, heard that it is part of the repertoire of Strandberg's group.

8. Through yet another web of causes and effects she finds herself at a specific point in space within the rather large campus area a few minutes before Moment X. Let's call it Point Y.

9. In the meantime, Lena, through her own web of cause and effect, moves about in the area so that at exactly the same moment she also finds herself at Point Y.

10. The person who found the sheets sees Lena, knows that she sings with the Strandberg group, and has the impulse to give her the sheets.

11. Lena gets the sheets in her hand. Without looking more closely she simply brings them with her, since she is on her way to the rehearsal room.

12. At Moment X minus two seconds Arne discovers that his sheets are missing and shouts "Where the hell are my sheets?"

13. At exactly Moment X, two seconds later, Lena opens the door, and the problem is solved almost at the same moment it occurred. A helpful little synchronistic pretzel in the flow of time. The funny thing is that it was in the oven already before the problem was known, and was ready to eat at exactly the right moment.

To a quantum physicist it is not an absurd notion that time can go backwards, and that an effect can occur before its cause. But to the rest of us, being used to seeing time as an arrow moving in a straight line from the past via the present to the future, it is pretty strange. I don't think the Field cares.

34 The big question

Why does the universe exist? Why does anything exist?
Would it not be more reasonable that nothing existed?

Friedrich von Schnelling

We are so used to being surrounded by cars, houses, mountains, trees, people, animals, taxes, televisions and everything else that we can see, touch or handle, we take it for granted that everything exists. It is only natural. It is just the way things are. But is it really so natural? Why does anything exist? And why do we human beings exist?

One thing is for sure: there does not exist an answer to that question. We can only speculate. It seems that in this universe opposites are each other's prerequisites. Long cannot exist without short, light cannot exist without dark, big cannot exist without small and so on. Everything is what it is in relation to its own opposite.

Thus it becomes obvious that Nothing cannot exist without Something.

Something simply must exist.

Now astronomers have found that even the vast emptiness

of space is not so empty. They have discovered that that there are enormous quantities of something called "dark matter". They are not quite sure what it is, only that there seems to be more dark matter than all the other known matter in galaxies, stars and planets put together. The name "dark matter" comes from the fact that we are still in the dark about just what it is, we are simply have not yet been "enlightened" about it.

As if that were not enough, it has now also been discovered that the universe is permeated by something even stranger, something called "dark energy". Even less is known about what that is; we know only that it is.

Some cosmologists have reached the conclusion that we know only about 4 per cent of what there is in the universe. The rest, 96 per cent of the universe in which we live, is unknown. In a world like that, how can we be absolutely sure of anything? There are definitely some big surprises awaiting us.

Some one hundred years ago people were convinced that soon all the mysteries of the universe would be solved. Just give science a little more time and then we would know. The universe was seen as a big clock-like machine, and it was just a matter of figuring out exactly how it worked.

Today, when we have reached farther out into space than ever before, the plot thickens. The pictures from the Hubble telescope and other observations pose more new questions than answers. The astronomer James Jeans said that the universe looks less and less like a big machine, and more and more like a big thought.

That big thought seems to have the ability to constantly create and destroy matter in a wild cosmic dance. I wouldn't be surprised if it also has a lot of fun doing it. Just look at all the strange things it has created here on Earth.

Nature abounds with the most amazing creatures – fish

with their own fishing rods to catch other fish, flowers disguised as insects to become pollinated, insects disguised as leafs or sticks to fool their enemies.

One of the most amazing is a beetle that is called the Bombardier beetle (*Brachinus crepitans*), since it has something similar to a cannon in its rear. With this "gun" the beetle can shoot at attacking enemies. It actually creates real explosions at a temperature of nearly 100 degrees Celsius. They even sound and issue smoke like an explosion.

This beetle's weapon is quite an advanced construction, with containers for chemicals, special glands that produce hydrochinon, hydrogen peroxide and certain enzymes necessary to create the explosives. There is an explosion chamber opening outwards, and a whole series of muscles and nerves especially designed for aiming and control.

When it is about to fire, it quickly mixes the two chemicals in the explosion chamber, each of which is by itself very hazardous to the beetle.

It then adds the necessary enzymes, simultaneously aiming the gun at the enemy, and poof! There goes the explosion. Not bad for a little beetle. One single mistake in one of the preparatory steps and the beetle would blow itself to pieces.

How can it be that this little creature exists at all? How could a blind coincidence have created this complicated defence system? Besides, there must be some kind of consciousness, or at least instinct, that can perfectly coordinate all the different steps for the cannon to work. It is hard to imagine that all this would have been possible without there being some sort of intention to begin with. And if so, where did that intention come from, and how did it create a piece of artillery in the rear of a beetle?

Another strange creature, one of the strangest, is called

slime mould (*Physarum polycephalum*). Science doesn´t quite know how to categorize it. It is not a fungus, nor a plant or an animal, but appears to be playing each of those roles at different times. What it is depends on when or where you see it. The closest to a definition so far places it in a category called *proteists*, organisms that nobody really knows how to describe further.

First, the slime mould is a single little cell. It starts growing and is transformed into an amoeba having the remarkable ability to crawl around. When it meets another amoeba sweet music occurs. But they are not about to make love and give birth to a cute litter of little amoebas. No, the two now literally become one. They unite their bodies into a bigger amoeba that keeps growing and eventually becomes one big slimy organism that crawls about in the forest in search of dead insects and other goodies. At that stage it is called a *plasmodium*. When it finds a delicious ant, it quickly grows one or two arms that stretch out to hug the ant, and soon the ant is no more.

Japanese researchers have recently found that it can even find its way through a labyrinth. It sends out arms in different directions to feel where there is an open passageway. Thus it seems to have a rudimentary form of intelligence.

Eventually, when it has gorged itself on dead insects and is satisfied, it looks for a nice dry spot in the forest, where it curls up and starts to dry out. Eventually small pliable stalks grow out of it with a kind of fruit at the end. When the fruits are ripe, little spores pop out, and a new cycle of life begins.

This strange being is thus acting first as a fungus, then as an animal, then as a plant. No wonder scientists are scratching their heads.

But perhaps strangest of all is the fact that during its lifetime it actually exists in two totally opposite states of being.

First as a single organism and then as a lot of totally separate individuals – each individual embodying the potential for a greater whole, and each whole embodying the potential for a lot of separate individuals.

No comparison (even if there are people who sometimes show certain similarities with a plasmodium), but what if the human mind has similar traits? What if it too contains the potential for a greater collective consciousness that in turn contains the potential for a lot of individual minds? In the same way that the wave is a part of the ocean and the ocean is a part of the wave. Perhaps each one of us is part of the Field and the Field is a part of us.

If the Field is independent of time and space and has created humans, Bombardier beetles, slime moulds and a million other strange things on this Earth, why then should it not be able to create meaningful events like synchronicities?

All of existence is synchronistic. The Big Bang, if indeed it occurred, was a synchronicity. If it had not happened exactly when it happened, at exactly that fraction of a second, the universe would have been totally different.

Your own existence is the result of synchronicity. If that particular sperm, out of millions of candidates, on that particular occasion, had not won the race to your mother´s egg, you would have been a totally different person.

Perhaps the fact that you are reading this particular book at this particular time is also a synchronicity, a meaningful coincidence.

It is, at least, very meaningful to me. Thank you.

35 *The Bermuda triangle*

Per Ohlson is a nice young man who recently received his PhD in biology at Stockholm University. His institution had a system of outside mentors for its students, and I was asked by his professor, Carl Folke, to be Per's mentor. This resulted in a series of interesting conversations up until he achieved his doctorate in 2003.

The year before his examination Per and his American wife Amy were going on vacation to Portugal. They were not interested in just lying about frying in the sun on a tourist beach. They wanted to experience the genuine Portugal, far from the tourist areas that are usually pretty similar wherever you go in the world.

After some searching they finally found a small house that they could rent in a remote little village high up in the mountains east of Porto.

They enjoyed the clear air, the beautiful landscape and the friendly villagers. Eventually they met the only other non-Portuguese person in the village at this time, a British antique dealer named Colin Cook. Colin had a summer house in the village that he visited as often as he could.

The evening before they were going home, they invited Colin for dinner. During the conversation he told them that he was fond of jazz and liked to play the drums. He also said he was originally from Bermuda, the British crown colony.

"Oh, what a coincidence," said Per. "I was just reading about Bermuda."

Per had brought along my autobiographical book *Reklown*, and had just read the chapter about my years in Bermuda.

"I have a friend who lived in Bermuda in the sixties," Per continued, "and he has written about that in a book I am just reading. I just read about it this morning."

Colin remembered that there had been a Swede there at the time. It may not be as strange as it sounds, considering that the local population of Bermuda is less than seventy thousand, and 75 per cent are black. There simply were not so many resident white people to keep track of in the rather segregated society that was Bermuda in the sixties. They were mostly Englishmen, such as you always find in the colonies, Americans working at the air force base Kindly Field, a handful of Germans in the restaurant business, and one young Swede working at the airport.

"What was his name?" asked Colin.

"Jan Cederquist."

"Oh yeah, I remember. I have actually played with him. We did some jam sessions together. He played the piano."

"No, Jan plays the double bass," said Per.

"But I remember, he played the piano, definitely."

Colin searched his memory and became more and more sure that he was right. It was the piano the Swede played. They couldn't quite agree, but both were actually right. I do play the double bass now, but in those days I did play the piano, and now and then I would sit in on jam sessions with like-minded people. Jazz was big in the sixties.

Per pulled out the book and read the names of several old

Bermudan friends I had mentioned, and Colin knew them all. He was much better updated than I was on their various fates and adventures in life.

I wonder what the statistical probability would be for Amy and Per to end up in that particular village of all the thousands of villages in the Portuguese countryside? That Colin Cook would be there for just the same two weeks they were. That they would meet. That he was from Bermuda. That Per had just read the chapter about Bermuda. And that Colin and I had actually played together.

Not that I can find any particular meaning in this, nor any connection to a known need or intention. But I do find it a rather remarkable little coincidence.

36 *The IKEA man*

Catherine and I were at IKEA to buy some kitchen equipment for our new summer house. It is when you are about to move to a new home or establish a new household that you realize what an enormous lot of stuff you are normally surrounded by. Our cart was filling up rapidly. It was pretty overloaded as we went towards the elevator to take us down to the cashiers' area.

Just as we got into the elevator a rather unpleasant-looking figure squeezed in with his cart. He was big and gross, with a black beard and a "hockey hairdo", short in the front and long on the neck. He did not look like a man of good intentions. I try not to be prejudiced, judging people by how they look, but I couldn't help feeling that this man was probably danger-ous. I was convinced we were sharing an elevator with a brutal torpedo from the criminal world.

Both Catherine and I felt uneasy, and it was with great relief that we rolled out of the elevator in the cashiers' area. We hurried as fast as the cart would allow us to get into one of the cashier's lines. It felt considerably safer – until we saw who was standing right behind us in the same line. The hockey hairdo, the torpedo!

Why had he chosen the same line as us? There were at least

ten others to choose from. And why had he chosen the same elevator? What evil intentions lurked behind that sinister face? And why had he selected us? Our discomfort grew. But what could he do in a crowded place like this? Would he make his move and rob us at the car in the car park? My almost paranoid fantasies ran amok. To keep some measure of control I slowly looked around, careful not to stare directly at him, just sort of casually pass my eyes over him.

He smiled. He actually smiled at me! I felt shivers down my spine. The man stood there with a sadistic just-you-wait kind of smile on his face. This was worse than a horror movie. This was for real. Catherine and I couldn't talk about it since he was too close, but our eye contact was communication enough. We felt the same thing.

I began planning for different options. Where would he make his move? He was probably armed, but even if he wasn't I wouldn't stand a chance against this gorilla. My puny orange belt in ju-jitsu would not be much to rely on against a three-hundred-pound trained torpedo.

This is crazy, I thought. This can't be happening. Here we are, peacefully going about our shopping at IKEA, and suddenly, out of the blue, we are exposed to an awful threat like this. Catherine and I exchanged frightened glances. The discomfort grew stronger. His very presence saturated the place with bad vibes.

Suddenly it was our turn with the cashier. We put piece after piece on the conveyor belt and the cashier registered the prices.

"That is four thousand two hundred," she said. I cautiously took out my wallet, trying to hide it from the eyes of the torpedo, and handed her my Eurocard.

"We don't take those cards."

"What? You don't take Eurocard?"

"No, only IKEA cards or cash."

I had only a hundred-kronor bill in my wallet, Catherine had two. For a moment I forgot the danger behind us. The sudden and unexpected money problem before us was too acute. What to do? Giving back all the stuff and coming back later for a new shopping spree was not a very attractive option. I was quite upset over this snooty attitude (to my mind) on the part of IKEA. My frustration was probably quite noticeable when I said: "Every shitty little shop in town accepts Eurocard. Why don´t you?"

"I haven't made the rules. I just do what I am told," said the cashier in a rather tired voice.

There we stood, frantically searching for a solution. Suddenly there was a deep voice behind us.

"You need dough?"

I quickly turned around. It was the gorilla! Totally confused, I stammered some sort of explanation.

"How much do you need?" He hauled a thick envelope from his breast pocket. My consternation was now total, but I had to answer him. My voice was cracked and hesitant when I stammered: "Well, we are short about four thousand."

He pulled out four thousand-kronor bills from the envelope and handed them to me. "Here you are."

"But ... but ... how ... must pay you back ... we must ..." I was totally incoherent and the whole department store whirled around me.

"You can fix that later."

With a feeling that this was totally unreal, I hesitantly handed the money over to the cashier. We packed our stuff in big IKEA bags while the torpedo calmly checked out. What would happen now? I could think of only one solution. The nearest cash machine was probably in the suburb a couple of kilometres away. I had to get there quickly and take out the money for him. I only hoped he would accept the idea.

"No problem. I can drive you," he said. "My car is pretty near by."

I tried to protest. The least I could do was to fix this myself, but my protests were lame and incoherent. "We'll take my car," he said firmly, and I didn't feel like arguing too much about it. Catherine was to wait with our bags at IKEA while the gorilla and I went out to the car park. I hoped it wasn't the last time I saw her. His vehicle was a large van.

I tried to figure out what his intentions could be. What was this strange situation all about anyway? It wouldn't make any sense for him to rob me and take the money from the cash machine since he would get it anyway. Would he take my card and force me to give him the code? Would he take my whole wallet with the other cards too? How should I handle this crazy situation?

I talked for a while about the weather and tried to figure out his intentions as we drove towards the square where the bank was. But I just couldn't read him.

We arrived at the square. I got out and walked to the cash machine. The bank was closed but the cash machine was working. The big man waited in his van. There was a limit to how much you could withdraw in one day and it was exactly four thousand. So all I had in my wallet now was four thousand one hundred. When I got back to the car I handed him all of it. The extra hundred was interest, I said.

"No, that's not necessary," he said. But I insisted, ever more confused about this figure. On our way back to IKEA I could not resist asking what he did for a living.

"Well," he said, "it varies."

I could well imagine.

Then he added, "Mostly I work with vegetables."

I began feeling pretty stupid. Slowly I realized that my whole fantasy about this man was perhaps totally misguided. I may have been much too quick to place him in a box, and as we drove back into the IKEA car park, he appeared to be a very nice and remarkably helpful person.

Maybe, considering his appearance, it was not so strange that we misjudged him. But it was certainly strange that he should be standing in just our line, just behind us, and just as we needed money hauled out his envelope asking how much we needed. It may have happened on some occasion that I have stood in a cashier's line and contributed a few kronor to a little old lady in front of me who was a bit short. But four thousand!

We shook hands and thanked him warmly for his help. It was obvious that angels do not always come with wings and golden hair. Catherine said it best: "You really are a true angel. But you sure don't look like one."

He laughed a jolly Santa Claus laugh as he walked to his car.

37 Everything is connected to everything else

*Small changes in one person's state of consciousness
can sometimes lead to great changes in the whole
society.*

Peter Russell

In chaos theory there is something called the "butterfly effect". It means that in a dynamic, unstable system, such as the global weather system, for example, a minuscule disturbance somewhere in the system can lead to big changes in the whole. It is theoretically possible that a butterfly flapping its wings in Rio could cause rain to fall in Newcastle. It may not be very probable, but it is entirely possible.

When a weather system is in a precarious balance, like a rotating football on the tip of my forefinger, it can develop in any direction. An almost unnoticeable impulse could be what tips the scale – such as the flapping wing of a butterfly.

It is true in politics too. Theresa LePore was working on a special project in Palm Beach, Florida, in the year 2000. Her job was to design the ballots that were to be used in the presidential election between George W. Bush and Al Gore.

A small impulse, a well-intentioned little idea, in Mrs LePore's mind made her increase the size of the typography. She thought that the slightly bigger letters would make it easier for voters to read the ballots, especially since there were many elderly, retired people in the region. A good and helpful thought, to be sure, but she happened to miss a small detail. For some reason she did not anticipate that the increased size of the letters would lead to an increase in size of the ballot papers. What had earlier been one page had to be redesigned and now became two.

A result of Mrs LePore's helpfulness was that 19,120 Democrat voters got confused and voted for both Al Gore and Pat Buchanan, another candidate. Their votes were thus declared invalid and ended up in the wastepaper basket.

A further 3,000 voters made another mistake. They thought they had voted for Al Gore, but in reality they had voted for Buchanan, so they were lost too. Altogether, in Palm Beach, Al Gore lost over twenty thousand votes of voters who thought they had voted for him.

If they had been counted, Al Gore would probably have become president instead of George W. Bush. How would that have influenced the destiny of the world? Would there have been wars in Iraq and Afghanistan? Would the many thousands of soldiers and civilians who have died in those wars still be alive? Would the Taliban still be in power in Afghanistan? Would Saddam Hussein still rule Iraq? Would all those who suffered under his oppression still be oppressed?

We will never know, but one thing is certain: that little butterfly that fluttered through the mind of Mrs LePore had quite an influence on history. That is why it is called the "Butterfly Ballot".

38 *Say it with music*

I had an impossible dream. It was to take bass lessons from the American bass player Red Mitchell, one of the living legends of the jazz world. Red had played his beautiful double bass with all the big names: Billie Holiday, Miles Davis, Dizzy Gillespie, Charlie Parker, all of them. He was the history of jazz personified and, most remarkably, he had moved to Stockholm.

I had of course heard and seen him at various concerts, and even occasionally seen him from my office window. My desk was placed in a bay from which I could see the street, even the house, where Red lived. It happened sometimes that I could see him come strolling along the street and I thought, *So close and yet so far.* I admired him a lot but felt that he was too big a star to be approached by a simple amateur like me. Although, in a rare moment of courage, I once did call his telephone number. A female American voice answered, rather unfriendly, almost aggressive. Red was on tour and would not be back for a month. I did not feel like calling again.

A year later Dick Nilson and I were at the Royal Viking Hotel to listen to a concert with Red and the piano player Horace Parlan. Dick had actually met Red when designing the cover for his latest record, so after the concert they met up to say hello. Of course, I tagged along. It was a big moment for me. I was introduced and got to shake hands with the legend. We exchanged some small talk and I managed to summon enough courage to ask whether he possibly gave lessons. I just could not miss this opportunity.

No, usually he didn't, only maybe on some rare occasions, but they were the exception. My disappointment was probably so visible that his resolve weakened a bit. "OK," he said, "maybe we could meet some time and talk about it." I wouldn't let go so easily, and we ended up setting a date for me to come and visit him.

I was very excited when a few days later I went to Red's apartment, and excitement turned into a mixture of fear and joy when he accepted me as an "exception". The situation improved further as my company was moving to a new building that happened to be right next to Red's house. It considerably simplified the logistics for me. Next to drummers, bass players have the heaviest burden when moving about. The bass is a big, cumbersome and vulnerable instrument. But it was not lugging the bass that made legs my shake as I rang the doorbell for my first lesson.

To begin with, Red wanted to get an idea of how I played. He placed me on his own bass chair and connected my bass to two gigantic loudspeakers reaching from floor to ceiling. He said sitting on a chair was preferable when playing the bass. "There are ten reasons for sitting," he said, "but not one for standing up."

He sat himself down at the grand piano and said: "Let's play something." Red was also an accomplished pianist, having actually started his musical career as a pianist with the American Air Force Big Band. But soon the double bass had become his main instrument and claim to fame. He belonged to the generation of bass players that had developed and renewed bass playing, and he had even given lessons to greats like Scott La Farrow and Gary Peacock. And now me. It felt totally unreal.

I was completely unable to move a finger. My inner dialogue went into high gear. Here I sit, a fumbling, inept amateur with my bass, and there sits one of the world's greatest bass players, a true star. He will just frown and think that I am hopeless. I haven't practised enough, I probably don't have enough talent. Oh my God, what am I doing here?

"What do you want to play?"

What should I say? Whatever I chose, Red would think that I chose it because I knew it well, and then it would sound like shit anyway, and he would realize that I was a hopeless case and …

"Let's play something you're comfortable with."

There was absolutely nothing I was comfortable with at that moment. I couldn't even play what little I could normally play. I began to panic.

Finally I realized that I had to tell him that I was paralysed from self-doubt, that I was just a lousy amateur who right now couldn't produce a single note.

Red smiled. "I know the feeling," he said, and told a story about once when he was playing the piano in a bar in Los Angeles. He was actually working as a bass player with the MGM orchestra under Henry Mancini, doing a lot of background music and themes for films and television shows. But that night in LA he was moonlighting, making some extra money, playing the piano in a bar.

Suddenly two well-known jazz personalities entered. They were no less than Oscar Peterson, one of the world's greatest piano players, and Ray Brown, one of the world's greatest bass players. They said hello and sat down right next to the piano.

"Sure, they were my buddies, but what I felt then is what you feel now." My deep freeze thawed somewhat.

Our lessons went on, a mixture of playing, instructions, anecdotes and increasingly philosophical discussions. In some lessons we could sit for hours talking about things other than music. Red was a very interesting person, an intelligent and creative observer of man and the world. Many of the lyrics he has written for different songs are very deep and artful, with an uncanny, perfectly happy marriage between notes and words.

I felt immensely privileged to be his student and partake of not only his immense knowledge of the bass, but also his wisdom and life experience. Gradually a warm friendship developed between us, and our conversations would often touch on the deeper questions of life. Such as, is there an afterlife? Is there a part of our consciousness or soul that survives our physical death?

Half-jokingly, but half-seriously, we made a deal. He who goes first – that's how we talked about death – would try to contact the other in order to confirm that there is indeed a continuation on the other side. "OK, it's a deal." We shook hands.

A few years passed. Red had moved back to the USA, to Portland, Oregon, with his new wife Diane. (It was not she but her unfriendly predecessor who had answered the phone that time. Diane was a very nice person.)

After a few months Red was back in Sweden, partly to attend a ceremony in which he was to receive the medal of honour, *Illis Qorum*, from the minister of culture, and partly to give a concert with the great guitar player Joe Pass. There was at the time a popular rock group called "The Grateful Dead". Red and Joe, who were both elderly gentlemen, jokingly called themselves "The Grateful Living". Nobody knew that it was only a matter of months for Red.

He told me he had been to the doctor because he had developed a pain in his left arm. The doctor had diagnosed angina pectoris. It worried him quite a bit. He liked his new life in Oregon. The jazz scene was lively, he was highly appreciated and had lots of gigs.

A few months had passed when one morning the phone rang. It was Red's son Eric, who told me that Red had suddenly passed away. I was deeply affected. Tears welled up. I felt a very personal loss and that the world had darkened a bit. It was the wrong timing. Red had so much more to give, I had so much more to learn. There was so much more I should have done, but never did, so much more I should have said, but never said.

That afternoon I became aware of a song that stubbornly played over and over in my head. It sometimes happens that you get a song in your head. It plays for a while, you are more or less aware of it, and then it fades away.

But this one was different. It was unusually stubborn and kept playing in a demanding sort of way. I just could not get rid of it. What tune was it? Oh yes, Red's composition, his examination work when he studied harmony with Dizzy Gillespie. A beautiful bossa nova with interesting and intricate chord sequences. He had named it "Talking".

Well, I thought, it's only natural that it should pop into my head today. My subconscious has probably dredged it up since Red was so much in my thoughts. I fell asleep that night with "Talking" still playing intensively in my head.

When I woke up the next morning the sadness was still there, but "Talking" had stopped. Instead there was another tune playing, just as stubbornly, just as demanding, and, just like "Talking", much more intensively than I was used to when I had a song in my head.

But I couldn't figure out which song this was. I recognized it as an old standard, but I didn't know the name of it and I had never played it myself.

It just kept playing and playing and would not let up. What the heck is it? What is the name of it?

Finally I had to call my piano-playing friend, Christer, who has a kind of computer mind, storing an amazing library of songs, chords, recordings and variations. Once in a while (or rather, too often), at a jam session, a tune might come up that I don't know. Then Christer takes a pen and paper and in two minutes he has written down the whole chord sequence. He has thus saved my face many times.

Now I needed his help again. I called him and over the phone I hummed that unknown melody that was playing so intensely in my head. What was it? Did he know it? Of course he did.

"Oh, that one," said Christer, and was silent for a few seconds. "It's 'I Get Along Without You Very Well'."

It struck me like lightning. Of course! Our agreement!

How would a genuine musician like Red Mitchell communicate, if not through music? I waved towards the heavens and said: "Thank you, Red. Good to know."

39 *Small coincidences*

It was a few months after Red's death. I was working on a project with the art director Ann Marie Wessman, and for some reason she mentioned Red Mitchell.

That got me started talking about Red, how much I liked and appreciated him, what a great guy he was.

At that moment the phone rang. It was Diane, Red's widow, calling from Portland, Oregon. I was a bit baffled and told her that she had called just as I was talking about Red. After I had hung up, Ann Marie also commented on the fact that Red's widow had called just as I was talking about him.

She had not finished the sentence when there was a knock on the door. In came Lars, a guy who had been working at the agency years before, and now had come visiting, just to say hello to his old buddies, whoever was still there. It was the first time he had been back since he left nine years previously. We shook hands. Good to see him, how was life?

The first thing he said was: "Too bad this thing with Red Mitchell."

Ann Marie and I looked at each other and almost burst out laughing. Lars looked a bit confused; had he said something funny?

I explained to him that he had just walked right into a

small but synchronistic little vortex that was all about Red Mitchell.

I was working late one evening and went down to a nearby restaurant with a colleague, Mike, to get a bite to eat. It was autumn, the days were growing shorter and darker, and the subject of autumn depression came up. It is a well-known syndrome in northern latitudes. I had recently read about SAD, Seasonally Affective Disorder, and began to show off my newly acquired knowledge.

Learning about SAD had given me an explanation for something I had been aware of since high school. Come autumn and I often became more introverted and lost some of the need for social interaction that is usually pretty active at that age. I sometimes even preferred going to the movies alone.

Now I had learnt that autumn depressions often have to do with a substance called melatonin, which is secreted by the pituitary gland. It is a small gland located in the middle of the brain, but it is still sensitive to light. When the days grow shorter in the autumn and there is less light, it secretes more melatonin, which makes you more sleepy. Some people also become more morose. This function exists in all mammals and is, for example, the reason why bears hibernate during winter.

I was holding forth to Mike and had just come to the influence of light. To illustrate, I stretched my arms out over the table in front of me and, slowly lowering them, I said: "And when the light goes down …"

At that exact moment the lights went out in the restaurant.

They soon came back on, but Mike gave me a strange look. I was just as surprised. We laughed at this funny coincidence, and I don't think it was anything more than just a coincidence. At least, I cannot read any deeper meaning into it. Should there be one I don't know what it would be. Perhaps just a sign of the humour of the universe.

After the first edition of this book was published in Sweden, I got many letters and emails from people who wanted to share their own experiences of synchronicity.

One lady told the following story, which connects to the little restaurant happening mentioned above. She was reading the book while travelling by train. Exactly as she was reading the sentence: "At that exact moment the lights went out in the restaurant ...", the lights went out in the train. She could hardly believe what was happening. The lights soon came back on, and she tried to find her way back to where she was in the book. As she reread "At that exact moment the lights went out in the restaurant ..." the lights went out in the train for the second time. Now she almost got scared. Eventually the lights came back on and she avoided reading that same sentence again. Her journey continued without further incident.

Sometimes you don't see things even if they are right in front of your eyes every day. My study is a combined library, music room and writer's den with a two-storey-high ceiling. A staircase winds up to a kind of shelf where I have my desk, computer, printer and all the stuff that goes with a place for writing. I walk up and down that staircase several times a day. Suddenly one day, going up, I saw it. An oak board is attached to one side as a kind of wood panel. It is kept in place by four screws sunk deep into the wood. I became aware of the four gaping holes where the screws were. Here is some unfinished business, I thought. They should have been plugged. Strange that I haven't noticed that before.

I need to get four round oak plugs of the right dimensions

to put in the holes, I thought. But where do I get them, what kind of store sells something like that? How do I find out? Who do I ask? Where can I call? The questions bubbled up, but dissolved quickly, pushed away by other, more pressing concerns. I would take care of it in due course. It was not, after all, a very big issue, and I was on my way up to the second floor of the house with other things on my mind.

When I reached the second floor I passed Catherine's desk. I froze in my tracks and stood for a moment, just staring.

There, in a little tray for pencils, lay four nice round oak plugs.

They fitted nicely.

When Catherine came home I told her the story and asked where in the world those four plugs had come from and why they were lying on her desk.

She had no idea.

My brother Torbjörn has one daughter, Camilla, from his first marriage, and another daughter, Elisabeth, from his second. Camilla was grown up, she had studied at UCLA and now worked as a copywriter with an advertising agency in Sweden. Elisabeth, who was eighteen, had just left home to start her own life. They met occasionally.

One day Camilla told Elisabeth that she and a friend were going on vacation to Asia. They were just going to travel around, going wherever their noses pointed, without any specific plan or itinerary. The only schedule they had to think about was their arrival in Singapore and their departure a few months later from Hong Kong. In between they would just move about at random in places like Malaysia, Indonesia and Bali.

When in Bali they visited the area that a few years later would be the scene of that horrific terror attack. It is a vast area for tourists with hundreds, perhaps thousands, of bars, restaurants and endless shopping malls.

That evening Camilla and her friend had dinner at a restaurant. After a while Camilla had to go to the ladies' room. When she stood washing her hands she saw in the mirror one of the toilet doors open. A girl came out, and Camilla had a feeling of total unreality.

The girl was her sister Elisabeth.

They were both astonished. Elisabeth had become so inspired by Camilla's journey that she had begun to organize one for herself and a friend. They had found a last-minute ticket to Bali.

She had no idea where Camilla would be; nor, of course, had Camilla herself. They had not communicated in any way since Camilla had left. And Asia is a pretty big place.

But here they were suddenly, not only in the same country, not only in the same city, but at the same restaurant, which is rather improbable. And even more improbable is that they should be there on the very same day at the very same time.

I guess the universe wanted them to meet.

40 Synchronicity and the Bible

Most people know the story from the Bible of how the Red Sea divided so that the Israelites could flee over to the other side, and how the water rushed back to drown the pursuing Egyptian army. Is it just fantasy or did it really happen?

There are now calculations that indicate that it actually could have really happened. That it could be an historical fact and a marvellous example of synchronicity.

The Bible tells of how the Israelites were trying to escape from their captivity in Egypt. They had set up camp at Pi-Hahirot, a place in the desert by the shores of the Red Sea. But the Egyptians were chasing them "with all of Pharaoh's horses, chariots and horsemen and his whole army". The Israelites were frightened as the Egyptians closed in on them, and they loudly complained to Moses, who had led them into this disaster. Then Moses received instructions from God about what to do. The Bible tells it thus:

And Moses stretched out his hand over the sea; and the Lord caused the sea to go back by a strong east wind all that night, and made the sea dry land, and the waters were divided.

And the children of Israel went into the midst of the sea upon the dry ground: and the waters were a wall unto them on their right hand, and on their left.

And the Egyptians pursued, and went in after them to the midst of the sea, even all Pharaoh's horses, his chariots, and his horsemen.

And it came to pass, that in the morning the Lord looked unto the host of the Egyptians through the pillar of fire and of the cloud, and troubled the host of the Egyptians.

And took off their chariot wheels, that they drove them heavily: so that the Egyptians said, Let us flee from the face of Israel; for the Lord fighteth for them against the Egyptians.

And the Lord said unto Moses, Stretch out thine hand over the sea, that the waters may come again upon the Egyptians, upon their chariots, and upon their horsemen.

And Moses stretched forth his hand over the sea, and the sea returned to his strength when the morning appeared; and the Egyptians fled against it; and the Lord overthrew the Egyptians in the midst of the sea.

And the waters returned, and covered the chariots, and the horsemen, and all the host of Pharaoh that came into the sea after them; there remained not so much as one of them.

Two Russian mathematicians, Naum Volzinger at the St Petersburg Institute of Oceanology, and his colleague, Alexei Androsov in Hamburg, have made interesting calculations using differential equations. The study took six months to complete and was published in the *Bulletin of the Russian Academy of Sciences*. It is entitled "Modelling of the Hydrodynamic Situation during the Exodus". This is the conclusion they arrived at:

There is a reef in the Red Sea exactly at the place where the Jews escaped the Egyptian army. It is 6.5 kilometres long and stretches from coast to coast. In ancient times the reef was bigger and reached closer to the surface than it does today. The Bible talks about "a strong east wind all that night".

So the two mathematicians worked out an equation incorporating wind speed, direction and other parameters to find out what conditions would be necessary for the reef to surface during low tide. What would be necessary for the reef to dry up, how long would it remain dry and how soon would the water return?

Volzinger, who is a specialist in maritime phenomena, tidal waves and flooding, calculated that if the wind blew from the east with a velocity of 30 metres per second, the reef would surface.

There were 600,000 Israelites who needed to cross over and he calculated that it would take them four hours. After a further half-hour the water would return, and that should be exactly when the Egyptian army was halfway across.

And the waters returned, and covered the chariots, and the horsemen, and all the host of Pharaoh that came into the sea after them; there remained not so much as one of them.

Thus there could be a clear physical, mathematical and scientific explanation for this strange tale from the Bible. But if so, is it not a powerful synchronicity that this natural phenomenon should occur at exactly the right moment when the Israelites were in desperate need of escaping their pursuers, and just as Moses stretched his hand out over the sea?

The event in itself may have a physiological explanation, but how do you explain its enormous significance? Perhaps there is something in Volzinger's own words: "I am convinced that God rules the world by the laws of physics."

41 Intuition

You can know the whole world without leaving your house. You can see the ways of heaven without looking out of the window.

Lao Tse

Does intuition exist? Learned minds have debated this question for thousands of years. There has never been any doubt in the Eastern tradition. One could perhaps see Lao Tse's words as a prophecy about television and the Internet, but he most likely meant something else. He most likely meant that human consciousness at a higher level is connected to everything else. It would then be perfectly possible to know things without having seen them with your eyes or heard them with your ears.

Western philosophers have a more divided opinion. The Roman philosopher Plotinus said that intuition was possibly of use in spiritual matters, but not for worldly affairs. The only thing that worked there was the discursive step-by-step-method. You could trust only logic and the intellect.

Spinoza on the other hand said that the highest form of

knowing demanded intuition. The intellect can give you only a fragmentary knowledge.

Henri Bergson agreed, and said that you could understand true reality only through intuition, which he even called a special organ of knowledge.

Schopenhauer confused things further with the idea that it is the intellect which gives us intuitive knowledge. It thus works according to the laws of logic. The problem is that intuition is subconscious and cannot be controlled.

Carl Jung called intuition an unconscious and irrational psychological process.

The sum of all these different views seems to be that there does in fact exist something that could be called intuition. Learned scholars may continue to argue about what it is. In the meantime, many people will continue to use it more or less consciously.

There is no doubt that the world view we are still conditioned by hails the intellect and logical thinking as our best ally in life's different situations. Be sensible, be rational, be logical, and you will be credited with intellectual ability. Small wonder that we usually rely on the intellect and miss the small, discreet inner voice of intuition. It is not even very linguistically sophisticated.

Intuition often communicates with just a vague notion, a feeling, an indefinite impression of some kind. And just as often the rational mind will jump in and say that it can't be so because ... The rational mind always wants to have its say, to judge, explain, interpret and sort things out. It is of course a very important faculty, and extremely useful in so many ways, but I am not sure it is superior to the emotional, to intuition.

There are expressions such as "emotional mumbo-jumbo" which contribute to limiting emotions to the world of soap operas. But emotions are much more than sadness, happiness, anger or fear. There are thousands of nuances, colours and chords; notions that are not easily packaged in ordinary words. There is a whole scale of different feelings between comfort and discomfort. You meet a person and feel slight discomfort without being able to put your finger on what is causing it. The person may be friendly and saying the right things, yet you do not feel quite comfortable. It could be your intuition trying to communicate something to you. More often than not, those kinds of feelings will prove to have some meaning.

Usually we do not act upon them, we prefer to shrug them off. But it might be wise to take them a little more seriously. The more we learn to notice them, and acknowledge them, the more information might become available to guide us in life. The accuracy of our inner compass will improve.

It could be big things, or small. Sometimes intuition can be very articulate. One evening I drove my son Oliver and his friend William to the movies, where they were to watch *The Lord of The Rings*. They got out of the car outside the cinema full of expectation, and as I turned the car around I saw them go through the entrance, eagerly gesturing.

I drove towards home. After about a kilometre, I suddenly had a notion, almost a certainty. They didn't get tickets! They didn't get in! The feeling was so strong and unexpected that without thinking I turned the car around and drove back towards the cinema. And, of course, immediately, my rational mind caught up and waved its finger. "What are you doing? This is totally irrational. This is silly. Of course they bought tickets in advance or at least made reservations. Why didn't you find out? Had you done that, you wouldn't be making a fool of yourself like this. This is embarrassing. Turn the car around and go home, for God's sake."

But for once my rational mind didn't win. I trusted my intuition and was soon back at the cinema.

Sure enough. Two disappointed teenagers stood there on the pavement wondering what to do now. "We didn't get any tickets."

I almost said: "Yes, I know."

The old world view might possibly agree that you can have "a gut feeling", and should it prove to be accurate it must be caused by one of two things: either "pure chance", or old knowledge and experiences stored in the subconscious being sent into your awareness in the form of a "gut feeling".

That is entirely possible. But I suspect that there is also something more to it. There might be a way of knowing that has nothing to do with anything previously learned or experienced. There is today quite a bit of research pointing in that direction.

One phenomenon that has been rather well studied is called "remote viewing". It is a kind of contact between human minds over great distances, and even the ability to "see" something in a totally unknown location thousands of miles away. Remote viewing is by now a well-documented phenomenon. It has, for instance, been researched for many years at the Stanford Research Institute, funded by American intelligence. The CIA were very interested in the possibility of being able to peep into the most secret Russian files from a comfortable chair at Langley.

The scientists Russell Targ and Hal Puthoff have described the research in a book entitled *Mind-Reach*, confirming that this phenomenon does in fact exist.

They are definitely neither flaky dreamers nor inept amateurs. Both are nuclear physicists and laser experts. Targ has, among other endeavours, participated in the construction of something called a "tunable plasma oscillator at microwave frequencies", and Puthoff has authored several books on quantum physics. They have been very careful to observe the strictest scientific protocols in their research on remote viewing. Even for those who hate leaving their comfort zone in the old world view, it is difficult to dismiss their research as unscientific.

Perhaps intuition could be explained by the fact that all information already exists in the Field, and that everybody is constantly connected to it, even if most people are not aware of it. With a bit of practice and focus, perhaps we could all sharpen our ability to derive important information from beyond the ordinary channels. I have experienced this myself.

42 *The struggle between intuition and intellect*

Once, in the 1970s, I participated in an experiment investigating ESP (extrasensory perception). It was organized by the Association for PsychoBioPhysics, a group of researchers who wanted to study special human abilities and limitations, but who were prohibited from carrying out certain experiments within their respective faculties as they were not quite in line with the "accepted paradigm". To challenge the accepted paradigm would be to risk future careers and funding, and perhaps being personally harassed by the establishment. Thus they had created this half-secret forum outside of academia, in order to be able to do research in their free time; research that the upholders of the old paradigm would find directly provocative. I had joined the association out of pure curiosity.

This particular experiment was led by the psychiatrist Nils Olof Jacobsson. We were a handful of voluntary subjects, each one sitting in a separate booth with pen and paper. In another room in the same building sat Matthew Manning, a young Brit who was noted for his abilities as a medium. Among other things, he had in his teens been subject to several poltergeist phenomena. Household utensils or other things would come flying though the air without anyone being there to throw them. This has been known to happen occasionally, often around an emotionally charged teenager, and it caused quite a few problems when Manning was attending boarding school. He was himself used to it, but the other boys in the dorm were terrified.

The phenomena eventually ceased and Manning now spent most of his time being a research subject. In this case the researchers had in advance put a large number of different pictures in unmarked and sealed envelopes. Neither Manning nor we had seen the pictures, or even the envelopes, beforehand.

Manning was to pick an envelope at random, open it, look at the picture and try to "send" it to us. We should in turn try to "see" or "feel" or in any other way get a notion of the picture and write down our impressions on paper. But we did not get any specific instructions on how to make ourselves open to receiving, beyond clearing out as much as possible of the usual chatter in our brains. It was very exciting.

The first picture was "sent". I tried to empty my mind of as much thought as I could, and waited for some kind of impression. Suddenly a pattern began to emerge before my inner eyes. I saw two thin parallel lines going from lower left to upper right. They were crossed at even intervals by shorter perpendicular lines.

What was it? The intellect immediately broke in to interpret. What could it be? Didn't it look like a railway, even if those lines were pretty thin? Yes, it must be a railway. The intellect was pretty satisfied with its interpretation and I wrote "railway" on the paper.

I should have asked the intellect to take it easy. If I hadn't immediately begun thinking and interpreting, perhaps the picture would have had time to develop. I have later learned that the greater mind often delivers its signals to normal consciousness in pieces that gradually grow into a whole picture. I had received only the first part.

The whole picture was of a tennis racket.

I had just begun to see some of the strings when the intellect stepped in to interpret, thereby closing down the reception. Had I remained open and in a receiving mode I might have got the rest too. My result was of course marked as a total miss.

At the next "broadcast" I got a picture of a curve or half-circle that seemed to be made of metal. At the same time I had a feeling that it had something to do with a lock. Again the intellect took charge. This must be part of a key. You just see the upper rounded part. Key it must be, and I felt sure when I wrote "key" on the paper.

The picture was of a padlock. What I had seen was the metal arch of a padlock. Had I cooled down, the rest of the padlock might have shown up. It was also marked as a miss.

The next "broadcast" didn't give me a picture at all but just a word.

The word "church" came flying almost audibly into my mind. Church? No, no, said the intellect, they would never use a symbol like that in an experiment like this. This study really has nothing to do with religion, they would surely avoid any such references. The Church is probably negative about this kind of thing anyway. No, it cannot be a church, decided the intellect, and had me write down something totally different. I have forgotten what surrogate I dreamed up.

How wrong the intellect was. The picture *was* of a church.

Another total miss was recorded. So right and yet so wrong. I was pretty frustrated afterwards, but had learned something important. The intellect is an excellent companion when you need to figure out how to use your new computer or fill out your tax return. But if you want to use your intuition better, you should keep the intellect at bay until the intuition has had its say.

The intellect is a good servant, but a lousy master.

43 *How I quit smoking without even trying*

I began smoking when I was around sixteen. All my buddies did it, Humphrey Bogart did it, all real men did it, and no one in those days, except for my mother, said anything about it being dangerous. It didn't always taste so good, but you got used to it.

The habit stayed with me and had me lighting up a cigarette at every break at school, every pause in army routine, every time the phone rang at the office, every time someone entered the room, after every cup of coffee, after every meal, and as some sort of consolation whenever a stressful thought appeared. I smoked between a half and one pack a day, more if there was a party.

As time passed, newspaper articles and suggestions that smoking might be hazardous to your health began to appear, and I guess I thought, like most smokers, that it would probably be a good idea to stop. But as every smoker knows, thinking about quitting and actually doing it are two very different things, so I kept on puffing.

Yet I stopped smoking for good within the span of a couple of minutes. It might even have been seconds. I am not sure since the incident was totally unexpected and very strange. It happened in 1974. I was undergoing a routine health check, not because I didn't feel well, but because we had a yearly check-up as a fringe benefit at work.

I was sitting in a chair and a nurse had just drawn two test tubes of blood from my arm. The tubes stood in a small stand on a table to my right. For some reason the nurse left the room. A vague impulse made me take one of the test tubes in my hand.

It was warm! Of course it was warm, since the blood had just come out of my body, but the thought struck me that heat is energy. The heat I feel in my hand right now is part of my own life energy! This thought acted as a kind of catapult for my consciousness. Suddenly I was somewhere else. The room, the chair, the test tube, everything was gone. I floated in some kind of black space where I saw my own blood as a separate being, a separate entity, with its own life, its own consciousness. This being was totally loving and had made it the whole purpose of its existence to keep me alive and healthy. Constantly delivering nutrients and oxygen to all parts of my body, and carrying away waste and poisons. Hour after hour, day after day, year after year. Never taking a vacation, never celebrating a holiday, never sleeping, just working, working, working, unselfishly, lovingly, and totally dedicated to my health and well-being.

I was deeply moved. Tears welled up and I felt an immense gratitude and love for this fantastic being. Then another picture appeared. I could somehow see how each cigarette I smoked made its job more difficult. Each puff was a spoke in the wheel, hampering the intensive, unselfish work of my blood, my best friend. Yet it just kept on working silently without complaining in its total dedication. I felt like an absolute idiot.

I asked sincerely for forgiveness. How could I have been so unbelievably stupid? It was totally absurd to have sucked on all those cigarettes. Never again! It was now absolutely unthinkable to light up even a single one.

Suddenly I was back in the chair. The world was once again the old, familiar one. But I was not. I was completely transformed into a non-smoker. I have no idea how long my visit to this other realm lasted, but the effect of it was to last forever. I haven't smoked since, and have never even felt the urge to.

Just in case, after the experience, I kept the half-full pack I had in my pocket, but it felt increasingly dry and filthy, and after a week I threw it away.

Nowadays, when I see the agony of smoking friends trying to quit, I wish I could transfer the intensity and meaning of my experience. But describing it now can only give a vague reflection of how it really was.

What did happen to me there in that chair? Could it be that my consciousness actually got access to another reality? Was it some kind of intervention by the Field? Or was it my subconscious, or intuition, which somehow created the experience to make me quit? I was obviously not strong or disciplined enough at the time to quit just through my own willpower.

Regardless of the explanation, I am immensely grateful. The experience has saved me a lot of both health and money.

44 *The return of the contact lens*

Off the coast of Croatia there is a beautiful island called Hvar. Something happened there that the architect Dusan Decermic and his girlfriend Dragana Spasogevic will never forget.

Dusan and Dragana lived and worked in London, but were on vacation in the little fishing village Sveta Nedelja on Hvar. The village is situated a little way up from the beach, with the top of a mountain towering in the background. Placing a village some distance from the shore was a common way to avoid the pirates who once made the shoreline unsafe. Nowadays it means only that the tourists have a slightly longer walk to the beach. But that is a small price to pay for the quiet, the idyll and the beauty of the landscape. And the tourists are usually not so plentiful that people are incapable of getting to know everybody else.

Dragana had limited eyesight and was dependent on strong, specially manufactured contact lenses to be able to enjoy the beautiful sights, the green mountain and the beach where she and Dusan used to swim.

One day they decided to go to another beach. They took the car and drove to a small secluded place about six kilometres from the village. There they enjoyed the sun, the sea and the beautiful little beach they had all to themselves.

They dived and swam and played in the warm water.

Suddenly Dragana popped her head out of the water and gave an anguished cry.

"I can't see! I lost one of my contacts in the sea!"

They started looking for it. Dragana was in despair. She had no reserves and her eyesight was considerably hampered. They searched frantically, but after a while they had to give up. What are the chances of finding a small transparent lens in a big sea? They drove back to the village. Their joy and holiday spirit were considerably subdued.

Dragana's situation was soon known and became the topic of the day in the little village. Poor Dragana. Such bad luck she had.

A few days later they were having dinner at the little village restaurant with its mixture of villagers and knowledgeable tourists. Only knowledgeable tourists find their way to Sveta Nedelja.

Another couple entered the restaurant. The lady saw Dragana and Dusan. She gave them a smile of recognition and walked straight up to their table. She held something up in her hand and asked:

"Is this your contact lens?"

Amazed, Dragana took it. She held it in her hand and looked, perplexed, at Dusan. Was this some kind of joke?

Still hesitant, with a well-practised movement she put the lens into her eye. She looked around, testing her eyesight, and gasped. She called out:

"Yes! Yes! It is my contact lens. I can see again." She jumped up and down, hugging both the lady and Dusan.

"Where in the world did you find it?"

The lady described how it had happened. She had been swimming at the village beach. As she got out of the water, heading for her sunlounger, she became aware of something glimmering on her bathing suit. She looked at it and thought at first it was a fish scale that had somehow stuck to her suit. Just as she was about to brush it away she stopped and looked again. Then she saw that it was not a fish scale but a contact lens. She was surprised but immediately recalled having heard about Dragana's calamity. Could it be hers?

The lens must have floated with some sea current the six kilometres from the place where Dragana lost it, and passed the village beach exactly at the time the lady was in the water, at exactly the spot where she was. In some way it attached itself to her bathing suit.

Maybe it is not so remarkable that a contact lens should float in salt water.

But how remarkable is it that it should float with a sea current in just that direction? That after the six kilometres it should be exactly off that beach, just as the lady took a dip? That she should pass the very spot where the lens was? That the lens should somehow stick to her bathing suit?

How easy is it to see a contact lens in the sea? How easy is it to make a contact lens stick to a bathing suit?

45 *Father and son*

Gregg Braden is an American scientist, author and speaker. He is a rare blend of computer expert, geologist and archaeologist, who researches, among other things, the connection between ancient wisdom (such as the Dead Sea Scrolls) and today's quantum physics. He has for many years searched high mountain villages, remote monasteries and hidden texts to uncover their timeless secrets.

I highly recommend a visit to his home page, www.gregg-braden.com.

I once heard Gregg tell a story that touched me so deeply that I would like to retell it here as I recall it. Just before this book went to press, however, I found out that the story was originally told by Yitta Halberstam and Judith Leventhal in a very powerful book, *Small Miracles: Extraordinary Coincidences from Everyday Life*. There was no time to contact the two authors for permission to tell their story, but it is my sincere hope that they will find it acceptable that I have tried to convey the main features of it here. Besides being a remarkable example of synchronicity, it has such a deep and profound message of forgiveness and love that I think deserves to be circulated as widely as possible.

It is about a Jewish family in the USA. The family lived

according to Jewish traditions, but as their son Joey grew up he felt that he did not want to follow the ancient Hebrew rules in his life. He wanted to form his own opinion of what was right and wrong, and how he should live his life in a meaningful way.

His father was very upset over his son's attitude. He had done everything to raise him in accordance with the traditions, and could not understand why Joey rejected them. The conflict was constantly present between father and son.

Joey longed to travel, see the world and try to find his own truth. One day he felt it was time. His parents tried to persuade him not to go, but they could not change his decision.

"I know, Dad, that you and Mom have done your best to raise me according to the tradition and what you feel is right. But it is time for me to go out in the world and find out for myself how it works and what is right and wrong. I have saved some money and I don't need very much. I will be OK."

"If you turn your back on our traditions and me, you are no longer my son!" said the father. "Then I have no son any more."

But Joey, who was strong and stubborn, resisted. "I am sorry, Dad, but this is what I have to do."

He went away. Having travelled around the world for some time, he eventually came to India. One day he was sitting in a small café, when suddenly an old schoolmate from his home town in the USA appeared. It was a warm reunion.

"I'm sorry about your dad," said the schoolmate.

"What do you mean?"

"Oh, didn't you know? Your dad passed away some time ago. It was so sad. He often talked about you."

Joey felt a chill coming over him. He regretted his stubbornness and decided immediately to go home.

Back in his home town he met many friends of the family.

They all said the same thing. His father had always talked about Joey, about how proud he was of his son who had had the courage to go out into the world to find his own truth, and how he admired and respected him for his independence.

Joey was deeply moved and grieved over not having seen his father again while he was still alive. He felt a strong pull back towards the Jewish tradition, and decided to make a kind of pilgrimage to visit its roots.

He went to Jerusalem and stood one day in front of the Western Wall – the ancient, holy wall, where people for centuries have stood and prayed. It is full of little crevices where the old mortar has fallen out, and people often write their prayers on little pieces of paper that they stick into the crevices.

Joey decided to do the same. On a piece of paper he spelled out his love and respect for his father, asked forgiveness for having been so stubborn, and prayed that God would bless his father's soul.

Just as he was folding the piece of paper to stick it into a crevice, another piece of paper fell out from another crevice and landed on the ground right by Joey's feet. He picked it up to stick it back into the wall, but a strange feeling came over him. He unfolded the little piece of paper. He seemed to recognize the handwriting. It looked just like his father's.

He began reading and suddenly felt the whole area start to swirl around him. It was his own father who had written on the paper. He expressed his love and respect for his son Joey, asked forgiveness for having been so stubborn and prayed that God would bless Joey's soul.

46 Pieces of the puzzle

Synchronicities are often associated with periods of transformation; for example, births, deaths, falling in love, psychotherapy, intense creative work, and even a change of profession.

F. David Peat

In his book *The Isaiah Effect*, Gregg Braden writes that we usually see time as linear and horizontal. We see it as a line from the past via the present to the future. For me it goes from left to right.

But time also has a vertical dimension. Each point, each moment on that horizontal line, is crossed by a vertical line that contains the potential for all imaginable and unimaginable events. Which ones actually occur in space–time reality might be affected by our emotional status. That could be an explanation for why some people seem to have all the luck, while others feel constantly haunted by bad luck.

Gustaf von Platen commented on it once. He told me about a person he knew well, and who always had negative expectations. This person very much wanted a certain professor's chair that was vacant. He applied but was sure that he would not get it, deeming the other applicants more qualified for the position. His fear made him eventually rescind his application in order to avoid the shame of being refused.

Eventually it turned out that several of the other candidates had, for various reasons, rescinded their applications too. If he had just kept his in place, he would have won that professor's chair. The flow of time contained several possibilities, but his negative expectations kept the one he desired from being actualized. He stopped himself from achieving his goal.

"I myself have always been lucky in life," said Gustaf, "and I think it is because I have never expected anything else." Most people who know him can confirm the fact that there always seems to be a positive atmosphere around him.

This simple story is quite easy to understand from a basic cause-and-effect perspective. But reality can be considerably stranger and more intricate.

One of the strangest things about us is our DNA. These very special spiralling molecules exist in every cell in every human, animal, plant, bacteria and virus. They carry hereditary information, determine our features and influence our health. Each person has a unique set of DNA, which is the reason why we all look different and are different individuals.

An American institution called the HeartMath Institute has, among other things, studied human DNA. They have found that the DNA spiral itself is not a rigid structure but rather flexible, and that it is influenced by the person's emotional state.

When a person is stressed, irritated, angry, frustrated or scared, their DNA spirals contract and become more rigid and tight. Also, some of the codes which enable communication with surrounding cells shut down. But when a person is relaxed and feels the opposite emotions, such as love, appreciation or gratitude, the DNA spirals also become more relaxed. They grow longer, unwind and reinitiate the whole spectrum of communication inside the cell.

These experiments were followed by studies in HIV-positive patients. It was discovered that positive feelings such as love, joy, gratitude and appreciation dramatically increased the patient's resistance to the virus.

This is strange enough, but other researchers have now discovered that the story of our DNA is even stranger. It seems that our DNA has an influence not only inside our bodies.

The Russian quantum biologist Vladimir Poponin made a remarkable discovery during a research project at the Russian Academy of Science. Together with his colleague Peter Gariaev he studied human DNA.

Poponin used a vacuum chamber, a container emptied of all matter, even air. The only thing present in the chamber was light, photons. Using a very sophisticated instrument called a laser photon correlation spectrometer (LPCS), they first studied the distribution of the light particles, the photons, in the vacuum chamber. As expected they were randomly and chaotically distributed all over the chamber. Then human DNA molecules were inserted.

Now came the first surprise. They found that the photons, the light particles, abandoned their chaotic state and organized themselves according to an energy field that seemed to surround the DNA molecules. The physical matter in the DNA molecules actually proved to exert an influence on the energy structure outside of themselves. This was against all accepted knowledge since the days of Newton. Yet there it was displayed on the scientists' instruments. And as if that weren't enough, the next surprise wasn't long in coming.

When they removed the DNA material from the vacuum chamber, the photons retained their new organization. It would have been "natural" for them to have returned to their chaotic state, since what had influenced them was no longer present. But they acted in a way that still defies explanation: they acted as if the DNA molecules were still there in the vacuum chamber.

This is a phenomenon that intrigues quite a few researchers today. It is called the "DNA phantom effect", and the experiment has been repeated in many laboratories with the same startling result.

The most interesting thing about Poponin and Gariaev's research was perhaps the fact that it proved beyond any doubt that our DNA actually can influence energy fields in our surroundings, and that the change is enduring. But the strangeness does not end there.

A military research laboratory in the USA has also experimented with human DNA. They performed a study designed by the well-known polygraph (lie detector) expert Cleve Backster. DNA was taken from leucocytes (white corpuscles that are part of the immune system) scraped from the mouth of a volunteer. The DNA material was placed in an instrument that measured and recorded electromagnetic changes in the molecules.

The donor was then placed in another room and subjected to various emotional stimuli, such as graphic war scenes, erotic pictures or comedy. He was in turn connected to instruments that monitored his emotional changes by measuring galvanic skin resistance (polygraph) and brain waves (EEG) – pretty accurate ways of measuring a person's emotional responses. These were in turn recorded on a graph thus illustrating the fluctuations in his emotional state.

When the two curves, the one showing the donor's emotional changes and the other showing the changes in the electromagnetic state of his DNA in another room, were compared, they coincided exactly. At exactly the same moment the donor had an emotional reaction, his DNA also changed.

The experiment was repeated with various subjects and the results were the same. There was some hitherto unknown form of communication between a person and his/her DNA. And it seemed to exist regardless of the distance between them. Backster later repeated the experiments with 360 miles between the donor and his/her DNA and got the same results. There was no time lag between the stimuli and the reaction in the DNA many miles away. This was measured with atomic clocks down to a fraction of a second. The reaction was instantaneous, making it impossible for some kind of signal, even with the speed of light, to have passed from donor to DNA. Something else was going on here independent of time and space. An example of what the quantum physicists call "non-locality".

Here we have two rather contemporary findings, scientifically verified, but still not scientifically explained:

1. DNA influences energy structures in the surrounding world.
2. A person's emotional state influences his/her DNA.

In other words, our emotions influence our surroundings, even if we think that they are just something that exists within our skulls. As a logical consequence of this kind of research, it may become evident that we influence our world, and what happens in our lives, in more ways than we have so far understood.

Perhaps this is yet another piece of the synchronistic puzzle.

47 Where are we heading?

God sleeps in the stone
dreams in the plant
moves in the animal
and wakes up in man

Sufi proverb

Every second millions of things happen in our bodies. Bacteria are killed, waste is hauled away, nutrients are taken care of, energy is produced, new cells are built, hormones are created, nails and hair are grown, possibilities for new children are prepared, electromagnetic impulses are sent, and lots of other processes take place, and at the same time you may be driving your car and having a conversation about politics. Everything is perfectly coordinated, second by second, perfectly synchronized so that the body as a whole will function as well as possible.

Synchronized by whom or by what? What computer, what kind of guiding system created by human beings, would be able to handle such an immensely complex task? It is definitely not my conscious self doing it. It must require a magnitude of information and communication that is far beyond what could take place in my limited little consciousness. Yet this whole magnificent process keeps going on, day by day, month by month, year by year. How is it possible?

I cannot understand it in any way other than to believe that there must be a field of information and energy existing both inside and outside of our physical body. The brain might be a relay station between the non-material field and the material body. The field exists on a level of reality that we as yet cannot understand, and it is probably there that all this perfect coordination is handled.

Since this field seems to have an incomprehensible ability to govern what happens in our physical bodies, why should it not also be able to influence what happens around us?

The field can at every second create millions of synchronistic events inside us. Then maybe it is not inconceivable that it could also create a few synchronistic events outside us.

It is no doubt a fantastic reality we live with. I cannot believe that you and I, and the unbelievably complex bodies we inhabit, should be just a blind and meaningless coincidence in a universe that in itself is just a cold and meaningless mass of dead matter hurtling around.

There must be another reality too.

The spiritual traditions have throughout history talked about that other reality in various ways. Science has not wanted to have anything to do with it, but has instead focused on the material reality. It has long seemed that the two were incompatible. The conflict between faith and knowledge has appeared impossible to reconcile. It has been a matter of either–or.

But something new seems to be happening. To quote Vaclav Havel again:

... the more accurately our organs and their functions, their inner structure and the biochemical reactions taking place in them, are described, the less we seem to understand the soul, the purpose and meaning of the system they form together and which we experience as our unique "me".

... Experts can explain to us anything in the objective world, yet we understand our lives less and less. The chasm between the rational and the spiritual, the external and the internal, the objective and the subjective, the technical and the moral, the universal and the unique, is getting deeper.

But there is hope, says Havel. And paradoxically, the inspiration comes from science. He points to two important theories. The *Anthropic Cosmological Principle* deals with the fact that out of all possible routes for its evolution, the universe chose just the one, the only one that made it possible for life to evolve. Talk about a meaningful coincidence.

Havel asks: "How can this be explained other than that the goal of the universe always has been to be able to see itself through our eyes?"

The other theory he talks about is the *Gaia Hypothesis*, which has been developed by the British scientist James Lovelock. Gaia is the old Greek name for the goddess of the planet, our Mother Earth. The Gaia Hypothesis says that the planet can actually be seen as a living entity. Gaia seems to constantly uphold certain conditions on Earth that make human life possible, such as the temperature and saline levels of the seas, conditions in the atmosphere and other things that according to natural laws should not be as balanced as they are.

The question is whether we humans are harming Gaia too much. "If we put her in too much danger she will do away with us in the higher interest of life itself," says Havel.

He ends with a plea to "respect the mystery of life, the mystery of the universe, the mystery of our own existence. Man's hope lies in accepting the existence of something that is greater than man himself."

I believe this is happening right now. More and more people seem prepared to accept that existence. Hopefully it will lead not to a new religion but to a synthesis between science and religion. The old differences between religion and science may at last be on their way to being overcome. Perhaps the two adversaries are cautiously beginning to turn to each other in a common endeavour to understand the mysteries of our existence. Perhaps it will turn out that both are equally valid.

Who knows what surprises await us within quantum physics, microbiology, brain research, chaos theory, non-linear dynamics and the like. Who knows where the growing spiritual curiosity will lead. According to Einstein a problem can never be solved on the level of consciousness where it occurred. Hopefully we are on our way towards a new level of consciousness that could solve the immense problems facing the world today. A consciousness that could lead to this world being a better place to live.

It is after all the human consciousness which governs what happens in the world – in economics, in politics, in the environment, not to mention our own personal lives. The strange thing is that the human consciousness has difficulty understanding the human consciousness.

The brain researcher and Nobel Prize laureate Roger Sperry once said: "Science has so far ignored a fundamental factor in our existence, almost omitted it completely, namely the human consciousness."

But this is about to change. Consciousness research has grown dramatically in recent years. Perhaps it is in this area that a new world view and new insights about ourselves are going to emerge. Perhaps human consciousness is about to take a quantum leap in its own evolution, perhaps even towards an insight that everything is basically consciousness, and that consciousness is what creates the material world and what happens in it. Then some of the veils around the mystery of synchronicity might be lifted.

It has been said that the human being is the world's most intelligent animal. I beg to differ. I think that we are rather the world's most stupid gods. What if we discover that we actually do have a godlike ability to influence our lives and thereby our world? That breakthrough may not be so far away.

Regardless of where or how the big discovery is being made, it will probably look like something that happened by coincidence.

But it will not have happened by chance.

48 *Two wolves*

I once heard the well-known motivational speaker and author Wayne Dyer tell the following story. I have forgotten when and where, but I loved it, and I hope that Wayne forgives me for telling it here as I remember it. I think it contains such a beautiful message for our time.

An old American Indian chief was sitting talking to his grandson. He was deeply mourning a tragedy that had occurred in the family.

"I feel as if I have two wolves fighting each other in my heart," he said. "One of them is violent, hateful and vindictive. The other one is loving, forgiving and compassionate."

The grandson asked: "Which wolf will win, Grandpa?"

"The one I feed."

Further reading

Anderson, Ken, *The Coincidence File*, Blandford, 1999

Belitz, Charlene, and Meg Lundstrom, *The Power of Flow: Practical Ways to Transform Your Life with Meaningful Coincidence*, Three Rivers Press, 1998

Braden, Gregg, *The Divine Matrix: Bridging Time, Space, Miracles, and Belief*, Hay House, 2008

Braden, Gregg, *The Isaiah Effect: Decoding the Lost Science of Prayer and Prophecy*, Three Rivers Press, 2001

Goodman, Nelson, *Of Mind and Other Matters*, Harvard University Press, 1984

Goswami, Amit, *The Self Aware Universe*, Tarcher/Putnam, 1995

Graff, Dale, *Tracks in the Psychic Wilderness*, Element Books Inc., 2000

Grof, Stanislav, and Hal Zina Bennett, *The Holotropic Mind*, HarperOne, 1993

Halberstam, Yitta, and Judith Leventhal, *Small Miracles: Extraordinary Coincidences from Everyday Life*, Adams Media Corp., 1997

Hawkins, David R., *Power vs Force: The Hidden Determinants of Human Behavior*, Hay House, 2002

Hopcke, Robert H., *There Are No Accidents*, Riverhead Hardcover, 1997

Jaworski, Joseph, *Synchronicity – the Inner Path of Leadership*, Berrett-Koehler Publishers, 1996

Joseph, Frank, *Synchronicity and You*, Element Books, 1999

Kamenetzky, Mario, *The Invisible Player: Consciousness as the Soul of Economic, Social and Political Life*, Park Street Press, 1999

Koestler, Arthur, *Janus: A Summing Up*, Hutchinson & Co., 1978

Lipton, Bruce, *The Biology of Belief*, Mountain of Love/Elite Books, 2005

Loye, David, *The Sphinx and the Rainbow: Brain, Mind and Future Vision*, New Science Library, 1983

McTaggart, Lynne, *The Field: The Quest for the Secret Force of the Universe*, HarperCollins, 2001

McTaggart, Lynne, *The Intention Experiment: Using Your Thoughts to Change Your Life and World*, Free Press, 2007

Mitchell, Edgar, *Psychic Exploration: A Challenge for Science*, G. P. Putnam's Sons, 1974

Peat, F. David, *Synchronicity: The Bridge Between Matter and Mind*, Bantam, 1987

Radin, Dean, *The Conscious Universe: The Scientific Truth of Psychic Phenomena*, Harper Edge, 1997

Radin, Dean, *Entangled Minds: Extrasensory Experiences in a Quantum Reality*, Paraview Pocket Books, 2006

Russell, Peter, *From Science to God: A Physicist's Journey into the Mystery of Consciousness*, New World Library, 2004

Schwartz, Gary E., and Linda G. Russek, *The Living Universe*, Hampton Roads Publishing, 1999

Sheldrake, Rupert, *The Sense of Being Stared At*, Random House, 2004

Targ, Russell, and Harold E. Puthoff, *Mind-Reach: Scientists Look at Psychic Abilities*, Hampton Roads, 2005

Tiller, William A., Walter E. Dibble and Michael J. Kohane, *Conscious Acts of Creation*, Pavior Publishing, 2001

Thurston, Mark A., *Synchronicity as Spiritual Guidance*, A.R.E. Press, 1997